VISUAL
THINKING

Empowering people & organizations through visual collaboration

Buro BRAND

Den Haag, The Netherlands

info@burobrand.nl

www.burobrand.nl

Author Willemien Brand

with essential input from:

Pieter Koene

Martijn Ars

Pieter Verheijen

BIS Publishers

Borneostraat 80-A, 1094 CP Amsterdam, The Netherlands

T +31 (0)20 515 02 30

bis@bispublishers.com

www.bispublishers.com

ISBN 978 90 6369 453 1

11th printing 2022

Willemien Brand

BISPUBLISHERS

VISUAL THINKING
CONTENTS ROADMAP

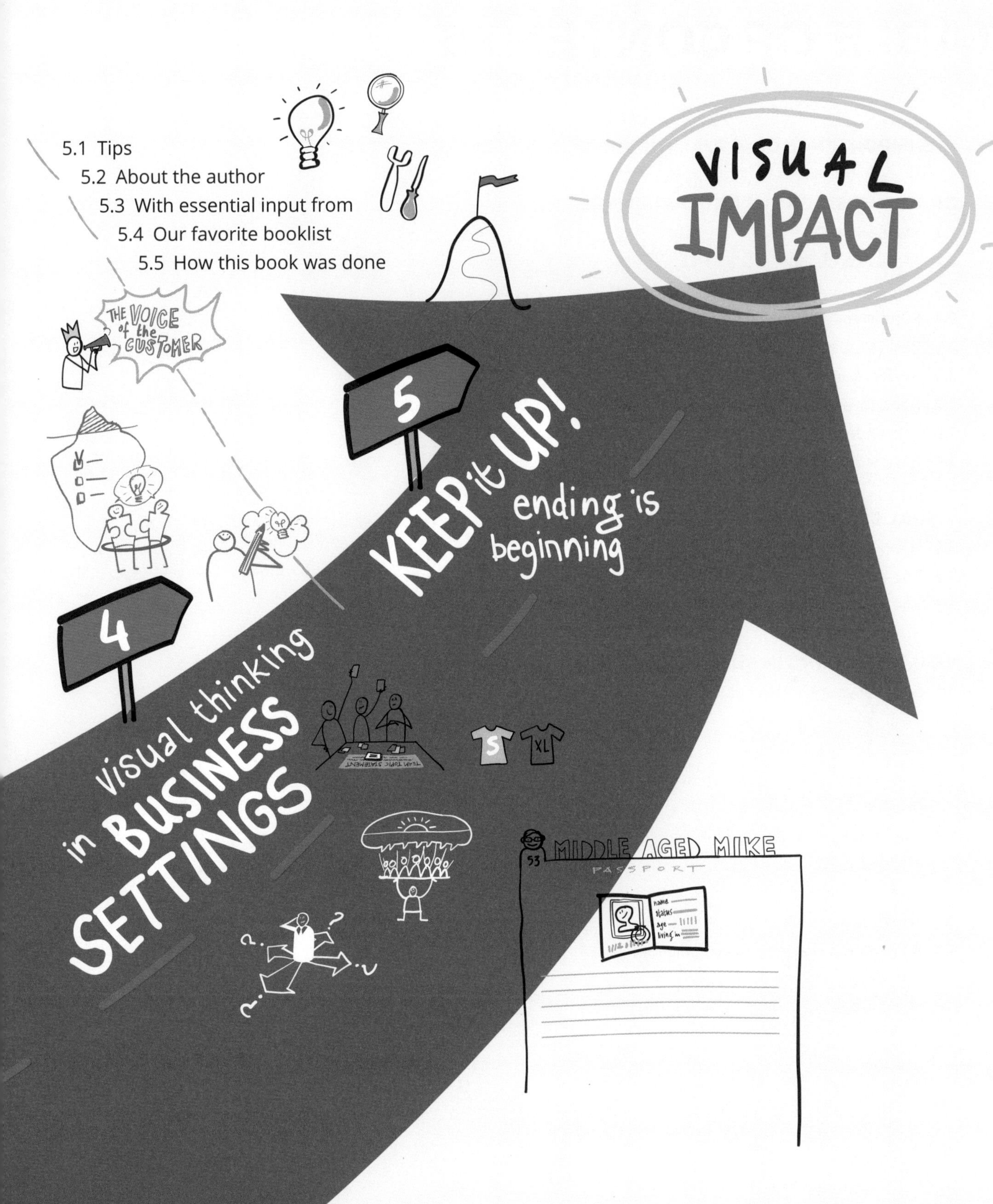
VISUAL IMPACT
THE VOICE of the CUSTOMER
5
KEEP it UP!
ending is beginning
4
Visual thinking in BUSINESS SETTINGS
S
XL
MIDDLE AGED MIKE
53
PASSPORT
name
status
age
living in

TABLE OF CONTENTS

IT'S DRAWING

NOT ROCKET SCIENCE

1. THE IMPORTANCE OF VISUAL THINKING

For me, drawing is not a hobby or even a job. It's a way of life! As a child I would draw non-stop. At the breakfast, lunch and dinner tables. At school, my naughty drawings made me popular while my visual notes of lessons helped me learn. Drawing enabled me to find my way through what sometimes felt like a complex maze of text. My sketches helped me to understand, summarize and distinguish the important from the mundane. After completing my degree at the Design Academy Eindhoven I became an industrial designer. But I wanted more freedom to create, so I started my own design company: "Buro BRAND | Visual Communication". I made a career out of my passion for making things look right and explaining things through visualization. The more I worked at this, the clearer it became that what comes naturally to me – visualizing processes to clarify and explain them – was a special gift and that I could share it and turn it into a service to help others. Every day I'm able to help other people unleash their creativity and use it to achieve better results in their work gives me joy and renews my passion for drawing.

When I met Pieter Koene, he quickly saw that my way of visual thinking goes far beyond a simple way of making sense of the world. Pieter taught me that my gift for visualizing concepts is a vital tool that can empower people, stimulate cooperation and boost innovation. When I fully grasped the enormous potential and impact of visualization, it made perfect sense for me to start teaching others how to use it in business settings.

This chapter explains why we wrote – and drew! – this book. It introduces the power of using images and visual thinking and it lays out how we will help you and give you the tools and skills you need to draw more and think visually.

WHY WE WROTE THIS BOOK

Visual thinking is not a skill for just a lucky few. Everybody is born with the ability to think in pictures, but only a few people nurture and develop this ability as they grow older. It's the same story with drawing. Everybody can draw, but the chances are you became discouraged as a child and neglected this skill. Sight is far and away the most important way we learn about the world around us. If you don't develop your drawing and visualization skills you will not unlock the full potential of the 75% of neurons in your brain used to process visuals.

This book empowers people and teams to unleash the full potential of their brains and use visuals to make more impact. It's not rocket science. We provide simple-to-use visual thinking and collaboration techniques as a foundation that can be built upon in different business settings and as a way of developing the confidence to draw.

For us, visual thinking is so much more than just practicing your drawing. We encourage people to use their own imagination, creativity and style. We want to inspire and teach people how they can make an impact in business settings by using drawings.

WHY USING IMAGE IS IMPORTANT

Why is visual thinking so important in business today? The speed of change has rapidly increased in recent years. Swiftly evolving consumer behavior, new regulations and emerging technological innovations mean companies have to adapt to high levels of volatility in their businesses.

Today, companies must find new ways of working to embrace this "new normal" in which uncertainty is the only real certainty.

Traditional ways of working within companies – characterized by high numbers of reporting layers, reams of written regulations and detailed planning – simply don't work in this increasingly dynamic environment. In fact, they actually stifle human creativity.

These days, companies need speed and agility to adapt quickly to changing circumstances. Companies are embracing new models such as the Agile Scrum, lean start-up and design thinking as a way of keeping pace with their ever-changing business environments.

All these new ways of working have one thing in common; they need a high degree of visual techniques to stimulate collaboration. These visual techniques improve the speed, creativity and effectiveness of teams as they collaborate in a dynamic environment.

The new work floor is a visual gallery populated by Kanban boards, user story maps and prototypes. These new ways of working mean that companies must develop their visual thinking talent. People need to develop the skills necessary to make an impact in this environment. This book will help you do just that.

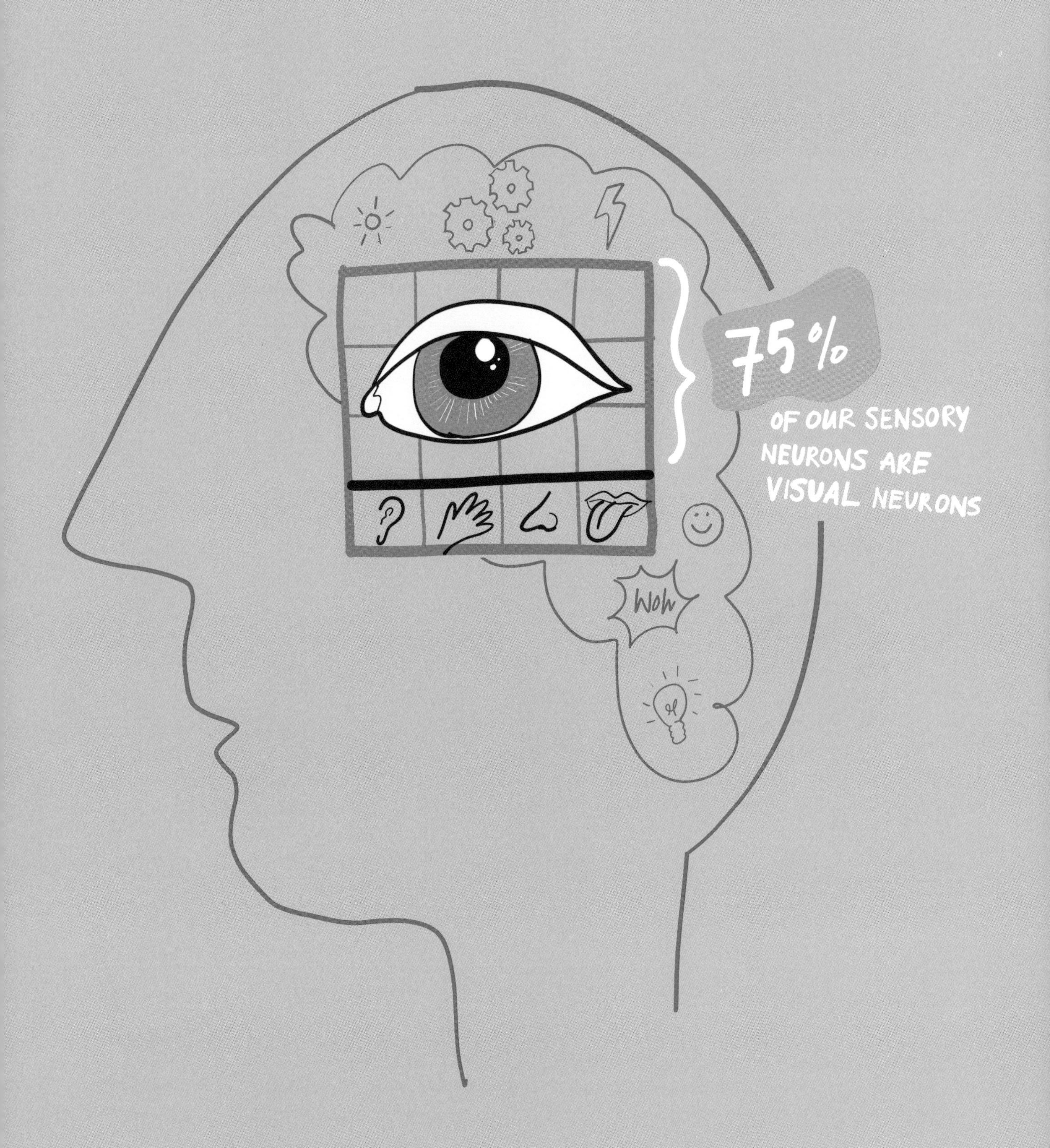
75%
OF OUR SENSORY NEURONS ARE VISUAL NEURONS
WOW

RESOURCE: DAN ROAM

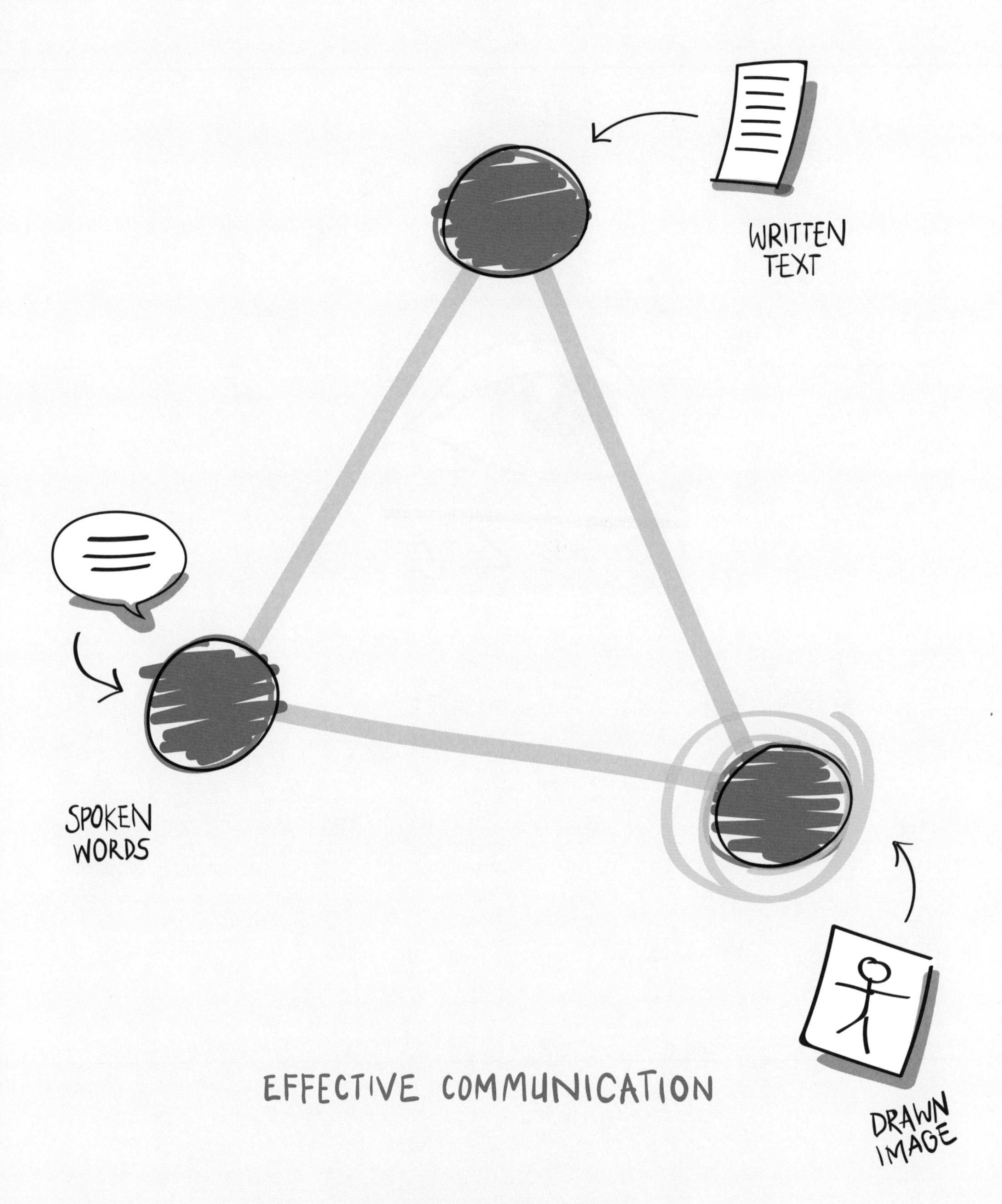

© Buro BRAND communication triangle

HOW THIS BOOK IS GOING TO HELP YOU

We don't want to limit ourselves to just teaching you a skill. We want this to be a practical handbook for your entire organization. It helps companies harness the power of drawn images alongside written and spoken words and body language.

The book has a simple message: You can do this! The lessons you learn on these pages can be used by your company as a standard for incorporating drawn images into your business.

It's actually exciting to use your own drawings in business communications. You need courage and a bit of audacity to create an image that will effectively visualize your ideas and priorities. But a few simple skills will enable you to start on this journey. We begin by teaching you basic skills. Just grab your notebook and draw everything we draw. Practice makes perfect – and even if it isn't perfect, don't worry. (You'll learn about the power of imperfection later!) Once you have mastered these basic skills we teach you how to blend your drawings into a visual story. Finally, in chapter 4, we put the theory into practice by providing straightforward visual techniques divided into real business settings.

WHAT HAPPENS WHEN YOU DRAW

Above all, you work at the intersection of image, spoken words and written text, where you maximize effectiveness and impact.

When you draw:

- You order your thoughts.
- Patterns and links become clear.
- Different perspectives open up.
- It can summarize the meeting.
- It can organize information.
- It simplifies.
- You keep on improving.
- You get new ideas.
- It opens people up.
- People stop focusing on small, irrelevant details.
- It makes the subject approachable.

On the next page you see an overview of why using images is important. At the beginning of our sessions and workshops we ask the participants why they think it is important and why it can add value. These are some of the many things they give back.

COMMUNICATE
FASTER

IMPACT on
TEAM
EFFECTIVENESS

simple steps

SHARING VISION

SPEAKING the
same LANGUAGE

MESSAGE
RECEIVED

drawing
is a GIFT !

involved
presentation

?
easily SUMMARIZE

AHA !!
IDEA GENERATING

BUILDING
TOGETHER

1+1=3

CLARIFY
PROCESSES

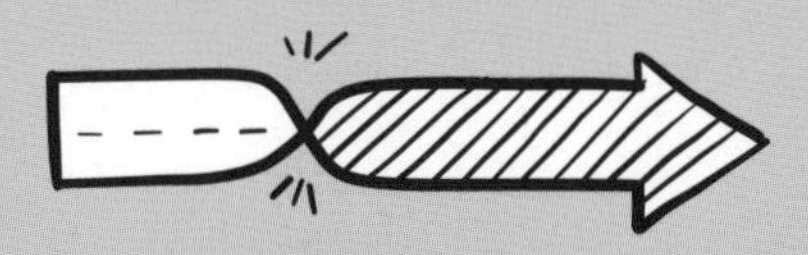

TRANSFORMATION

approachable

hidden links

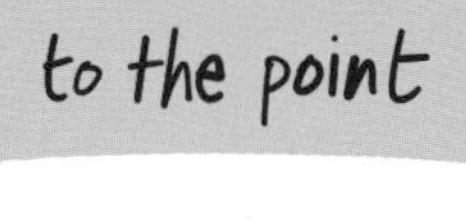

UNLOCKING
CREATIVE POWER

DARE TO
DRAW!

2. DRAW! BASIC SKILLS AND GUIDELINES

People will enjoy watching you draw and value your drawings. We hear it all the time: 'I can't draw.' But the good news is, it's not about the quality of your drawing, it's about connecting with each other through drawings.
So this chapter is all about giving you the skills that will help you communicate and connect through your drawings.

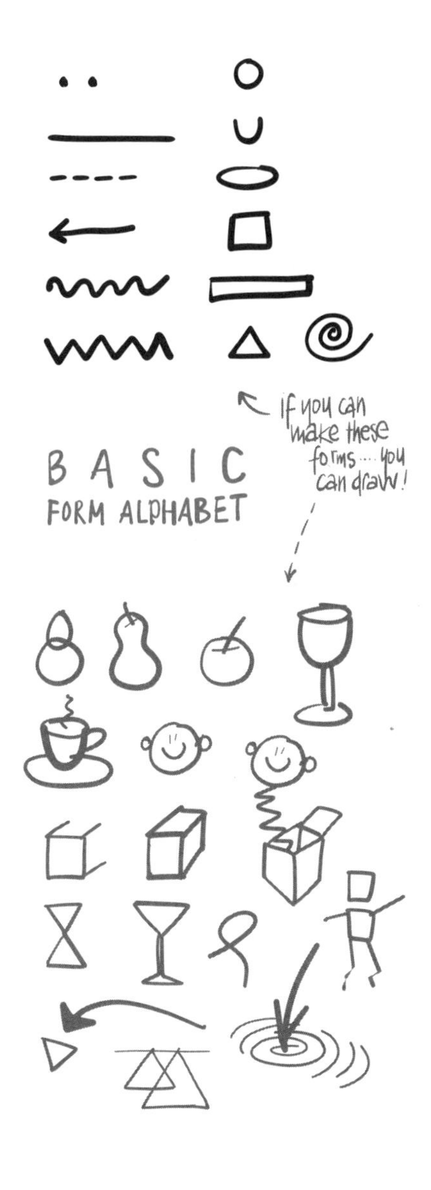

What will you learn in this chapter?

- Develop the courage to draw. If you can write you can draw! Overcome fear of failure!
- Tell your story in a visual and authentic way.
- Think visually. Break down technical jargon into simple and clear images.

MINIMAL EFFORT, MAXIMUM OUTCOME

Drawing is all about courage.
The best way to beat fear of failure is by just doing it. Make a start by putting lines on paper like a child. Draw headfooters or tadpole people. They may not be realistic, but the powerful and convincing lines give them credibility.

Mix up the speed of drawing. Don't try to draw as fast as you speak. Go fast for flow, for detail go slow.

Make sure to close corners and circles! Don't leave shapes open. Closing them will solidify your illustration and make your drawings easier on the eye. For example, don't let legs dangle somewhere below the body, make sure you attach them!

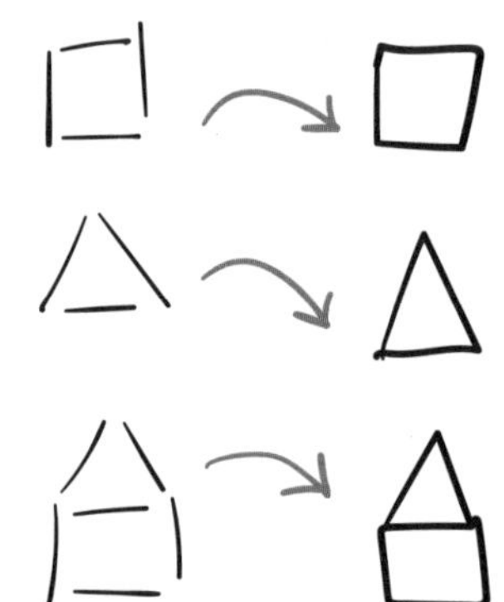

Fewer lines mean more impact. Sounds simple, right? But it is very tempting to keep adding lines. This just complicates your drawing and diminishes its visual impact. Keep it simple, stupid!

#TIP:
ask yourself which lines are necessary to communicate 'tree'...

Illustration of a tree, full of detail.

Illustration of the idea of a tree.

Illustration of a useful tree metaphor.

FEWER lines
MORE
IMPACT

2.1 MATERIALS & COLORS

Here are some of our favorite tools of the drawing trade. We love using black and especially gray markers for sketching and applying shadow. We recommend Neuland markers for use on flipovers or flipcharts. They are very smooth and their ink doesn't bleed through the paper. The black one-liner (in an orange body) doesn't stain if you go over the lines with a different color. We are also huge fans of using broad chisel-tipped markers to easily apply both thick and thin lines in your drawings. Using different weights of line and a limited color palette gives your drawing strength. Less is more! Using too many colors will result in an unbalanced image with too many focal points. There are no such things as mistakes. Just turn to a new page and try again!

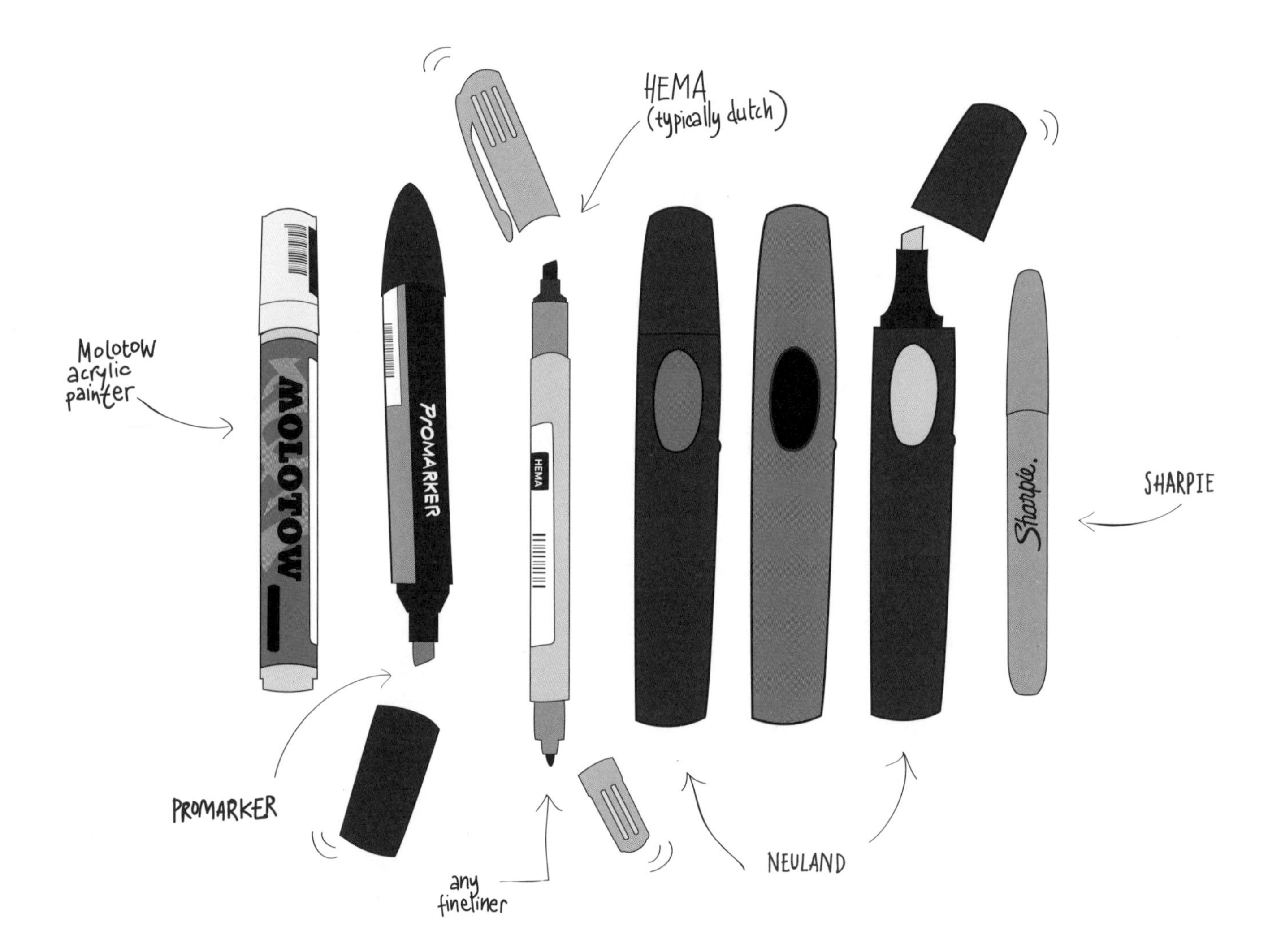

BLACK; THIN, THICK AND GREY

You can create maximum impact with a minimum of effort. You basically only need a combination of black and gray, with thick and thin lines. Varying line thickness and using black and gray is all you need to create an appealing and layered composition.

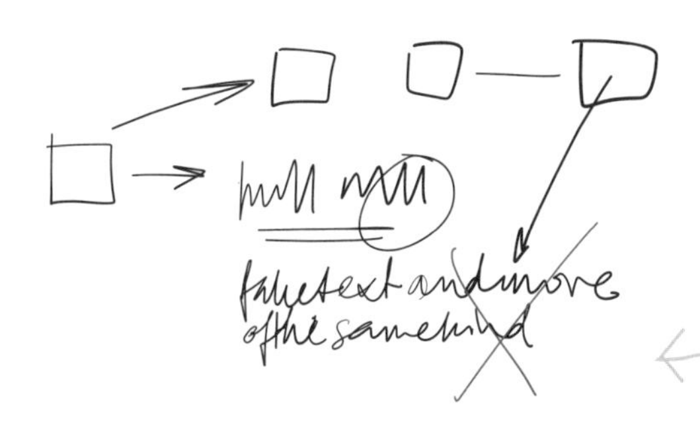

We see a lot of process maps like these. Yawn! Using just one color and line width makes them totally boring!

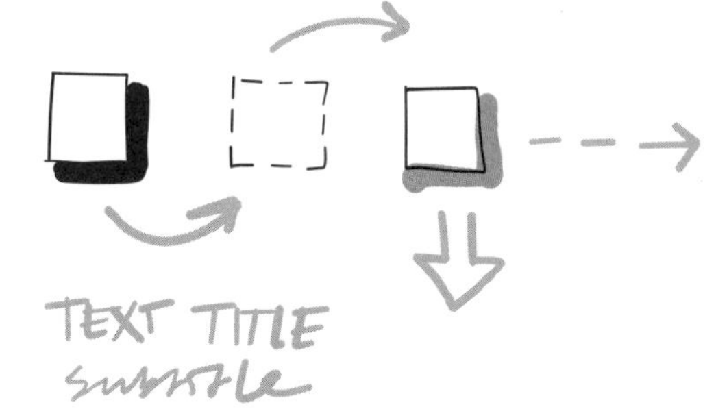

BIG TIP: Draw your connection lines and arrows in grey for more hierarchy.

Gray can be used for either a sketching line or for shadowing. If you use gray as a sketch line, you can complete the drawing by tracing the line with black. Finally, use color to highlight important elements.

TIP: Start with grey. ALWAYS. Conclude with black (thin lines) and use colour to emphasize highlights.

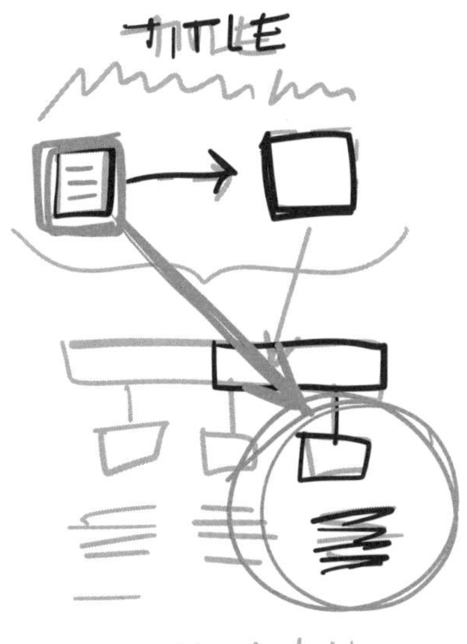

2.2 FACIAL EXPRESSIONS

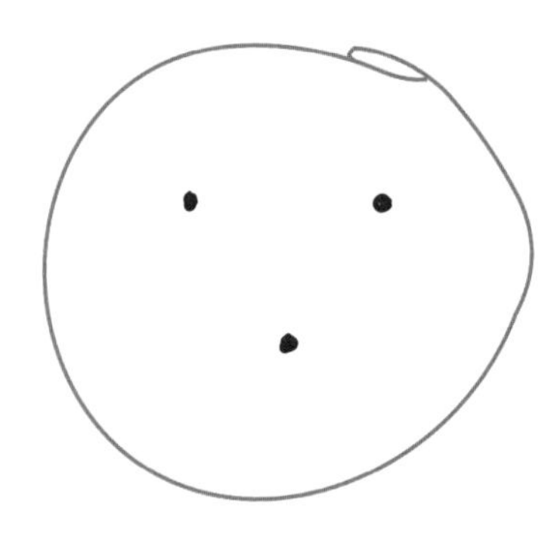

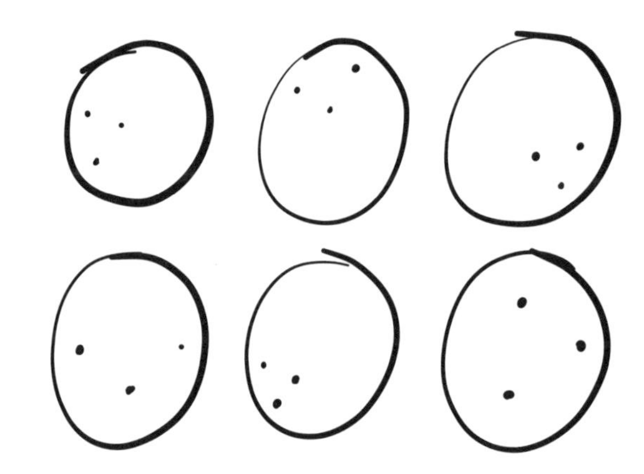

Your brain only needs three dots to recognize a face. Try it yourself by drawing a few potato heads with three randomly placed dots inside. They've created a facial expression simply because of their positions relative to each other.

Putting the dots on different sides of the face defines a viewing direction. Try to enhance your face by using different mouths and eyebrows.

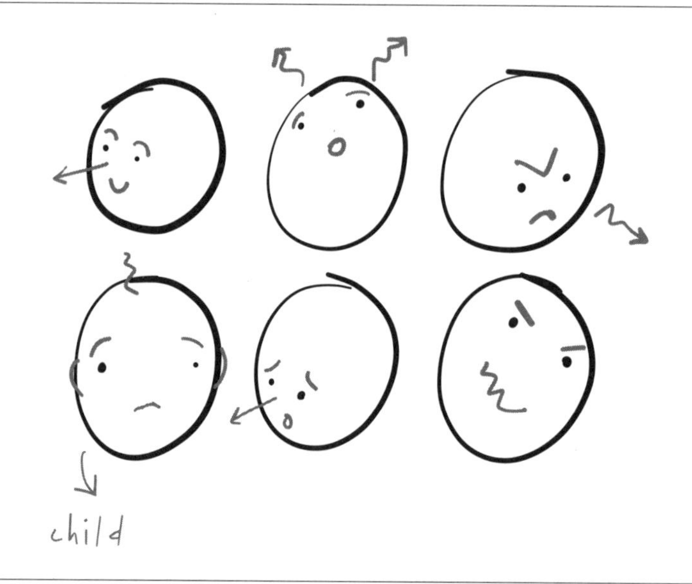

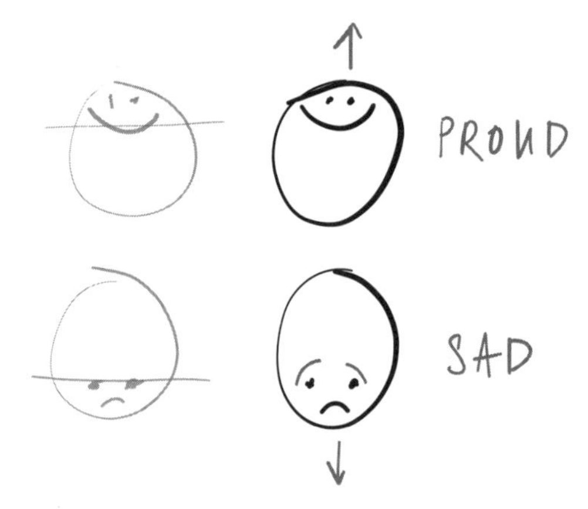

MY FAVORITE EMOTICON

MY FAVORITE WHATSAPP EMOTICON

A great way of practicing facial expressions is copying your favorite emoticons. Try drawing one from memory and check if it matches reality. Copying is learning!

neutral

try it yourself!

agreement good mood — sad — question uncertain — surprise frightened

shyness — embarrassment — confused — dreaming — irony

meanness — mad — humbug — disrespect

INTERACTION

A great way of drawing interaction is by using text balloons. The shape can tell a lot about the type of interaction. Drawing or writing in them can provide more emphasis.

Drawing figures with your text balloons can really add detail to the interaction. The posture of your figure along with a facial expression and well-placed limbs can tell a story in itself.

TIP: Use color only to highlight an accessory, not for main lines.

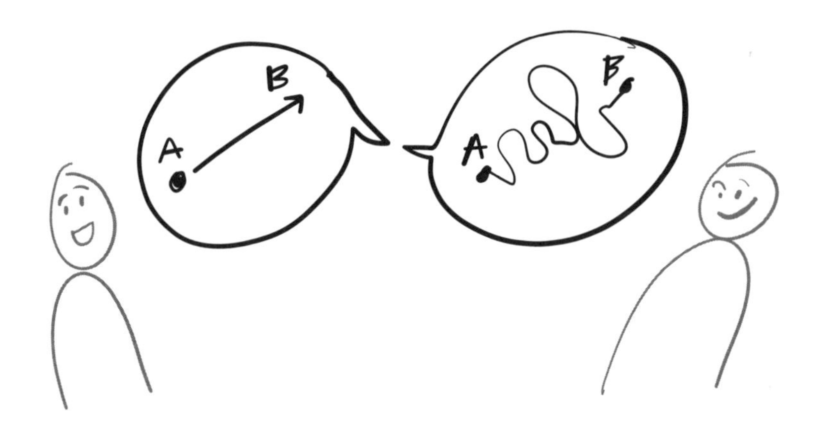

2.3 DRAWING PEOPLE GOING PLACES

Now you know how to communicate all sorts of expressions, let's see what figure positions can show. We usually use an oval shape directly underneath the head. If you feel like your body should be square, bold or geometric; go for it!

We love zigzags! They're easy to draw and make a great hand. If you want to make a figure with a hand at his sides or on his head, draw a turned 'V' with a little 'M' on the end. If you want to make a pointed finger, thumbs up or down, just take a look at your own hand and try to draw it. The fingers don't need to close in on to the stick that forms the arm, just leave a little space.

NOTE: Arms and legs do not grow out of the middle of your body (unless you want to make a skirt).

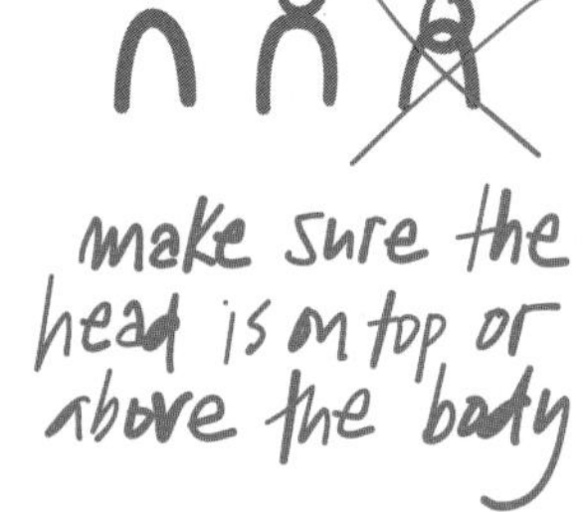
make sure the
head is on top or
above the body

movement lines in grey!

If you want to add movement to your body, start with the torso. This gives your body the right angle onto which you can attach limbs and a head.

TIP: Sad people are bent over, shoulders up, face down. Happy or proud people have their shoulders back, face up and hands at their sides.

A great exercise to practise postures is making your own pitfall. Try to make your own visual story including a few figures.

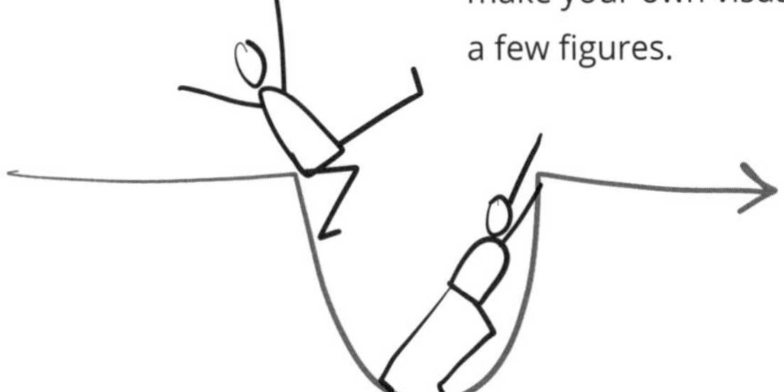

MULTIPLE PEOPLE

Creating a team is just as easy.

If you simply draw a big wave (the same way as for making flowers and clouds) you only have to put some heads on them to create multiple people.

Give them facial expressions, text-balloons and other accessories and your story has begun.

Give your co-workers a different T-shirt to show their job positions. Decide which pattern represents each position. Be consistent when drawing a visual story.

Drawing a manager doesn't have to be difficult; just give him or her a nice tie! We know lots of companies don't work like this anymore but untill there is a new globally accepted icon for manager why not stick to the tie?

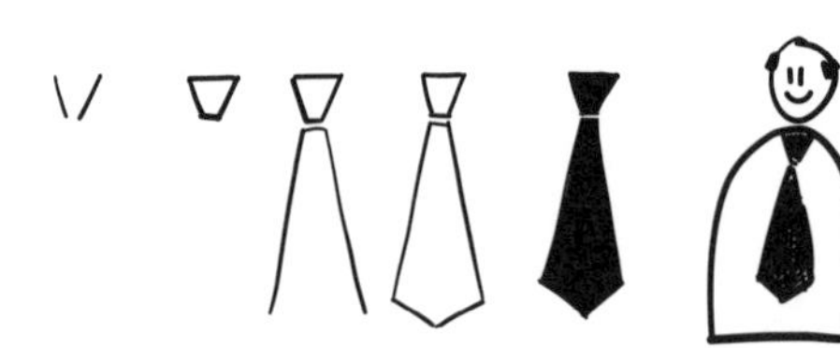

TIP: Male and female managers can wear a tie!

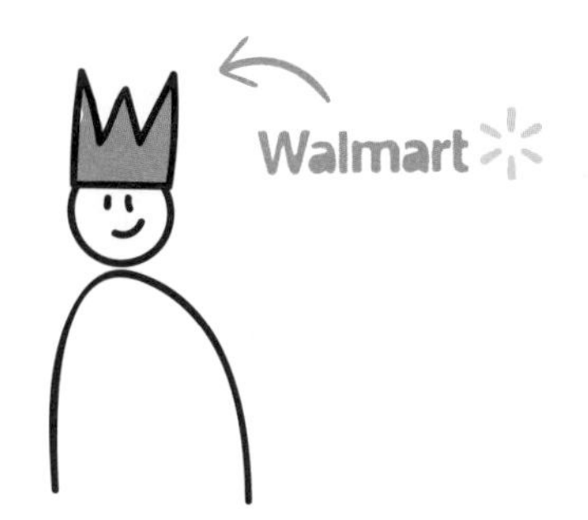

Customer is king! If you want to draw one, just make a figure and give it a crown. Colour can also tell a story; a yellow crown can be a normal client but by giving the crown the colour of your company it is YOUR client.

TIP: Draw the crown slowly.

BASIC BUSINESS ICONS AND VISUAL STORYTELLING

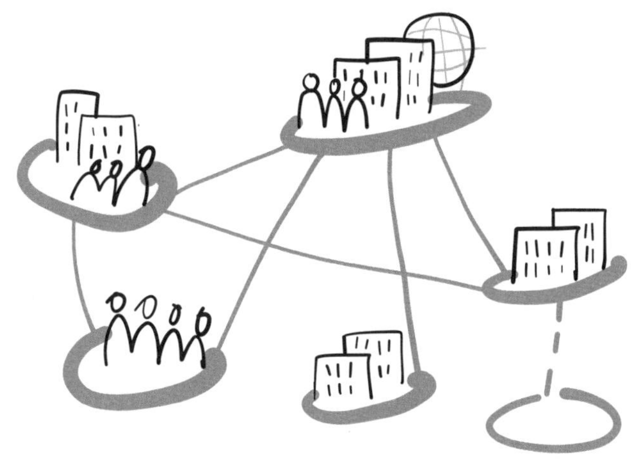

The skills you have gathered now make creating a visual story so much easier. Now try combining some icons and using arrows and lines to connect several drawings.

TIP: Slowly draw small vertical stripes in a rhythmic order to make windows in buildings.

DRUM UP THE COURAGE TO DRAW

CHARACTERS

What if you have to draw a specific person? Just draw their hair. Easy! Does this person wear glasses? Draw them, too.

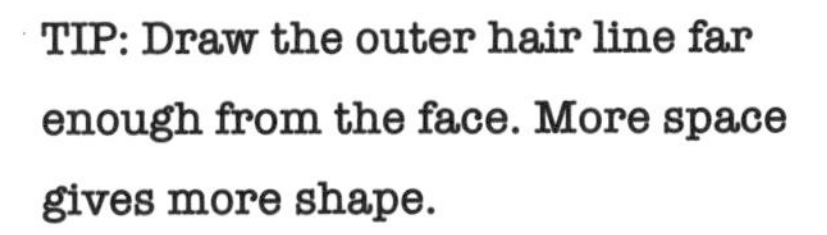

TIP: Draw the outer hair line far enough from the face. More space gives more shape.

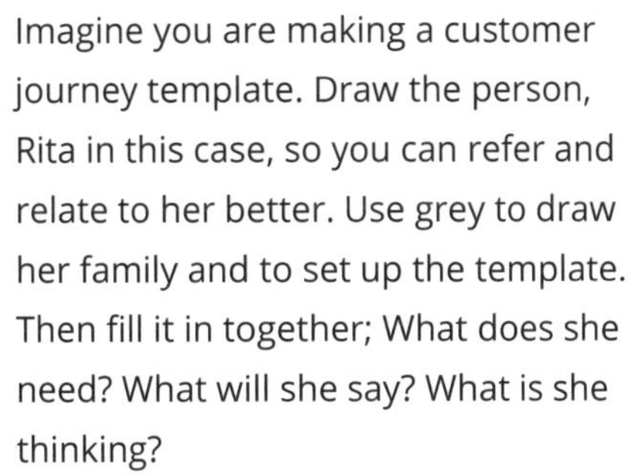

Imagine you are making a customer journey template. Draw the person, Rita in this case, so you can refer and relate to her better. Use grey to draw her family and to set up the template. Then fill it in together; What does she need? What will she say? What is she thinking?

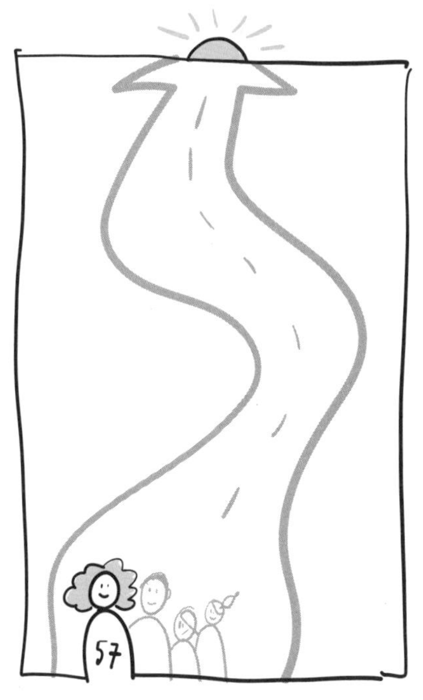

2.4 PUTTING VISUAL THINKING INTO PRACTICE

IT

guide

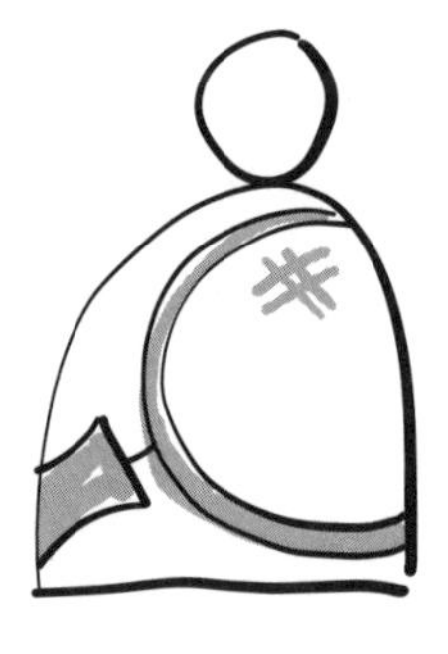

analyst

road manager

customer journey expert

innovation

coach

How hard is it to draw a complicated idea in a small space like a simple figure or a text balloon? If you want to draw your occupation, the key is to keep things simple. Try imagining how you would explain your job to a small child. Use metaphors, make it small and try to draw it in the body of your figure.

Try it yourself: how would you vizualize your job?

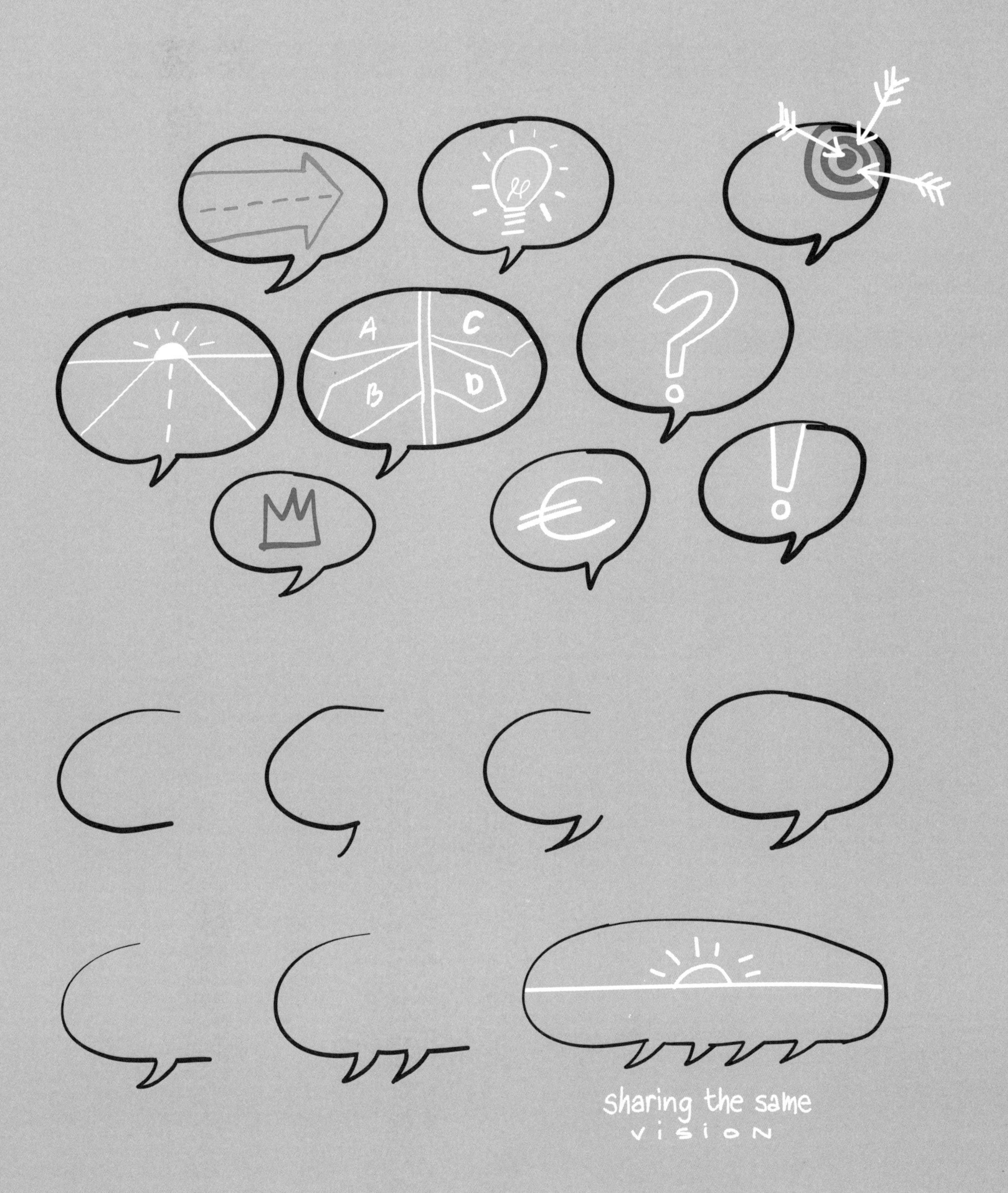
A
C
B
D
sharing the same
VISION

2.5 BASIC SHAPES & SHADOWS

If you want to spice up your drawing, just add shadow. It doesn't have to be perfect; all you need are some simple gray accents.

Shadows of round objects don't touch the side line because round objects reflect light. Keep that in mind while creating an arty piece of fruit or vegetable.

TIP: The basic shadow rule we always apply; draw your shadow consistently left or right, and at the bottom of your object.

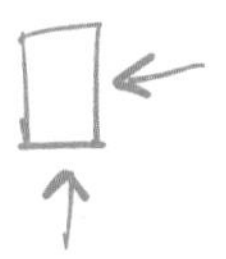

If you draw a 3D cube you can either fill in only one shadow side (the darkest one) or two if you have extra time and 2 markers.

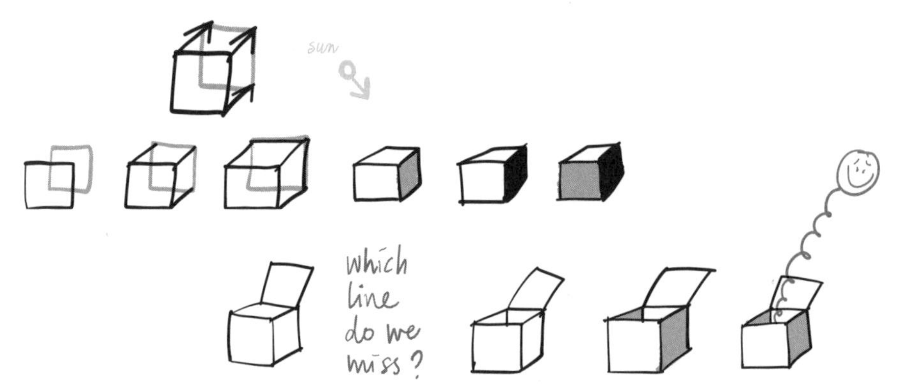

Once you have a basic cube, it is only a small step to create a box. Don't forget the extra shadow point on the inside!

You can easily create a 3D illusion with overlapping objects. Add shadows on the overlapping area and use thin and thick lines for extra impact.

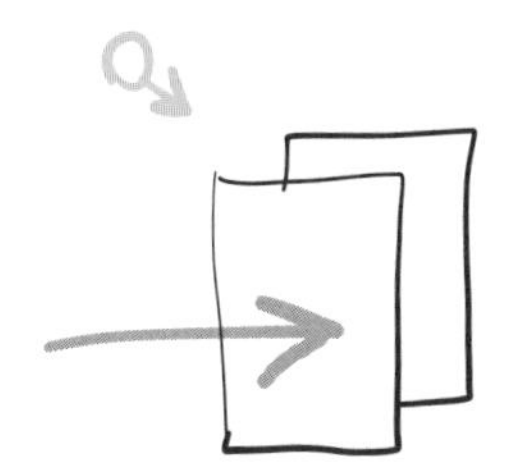

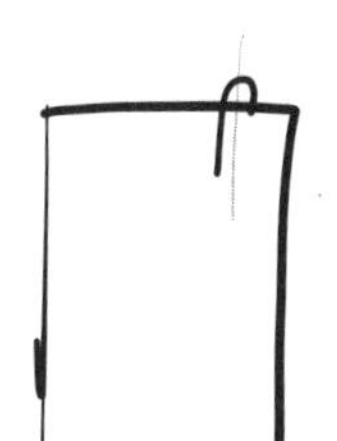

use thin
& thick
lines

OFFER

Shadow use:
always choose
for one side
and the bottom

never use dull
checkboxes
again!

Using a cylinder shape, you can create 3D objects such as glasses, cups and vases. Always start with the flat circle at the top and work your way down.

Put the shadow on the side and don't let it touch the outline because this is also a round object. If you are not sure about your lines, start in gray and finish your sketch with black.

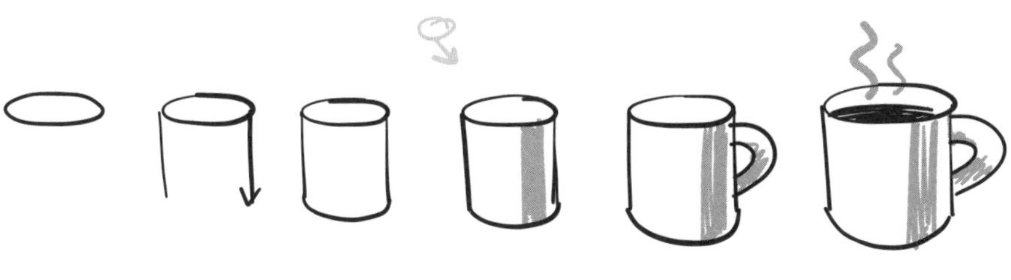

don't
fill
it
to
the
top

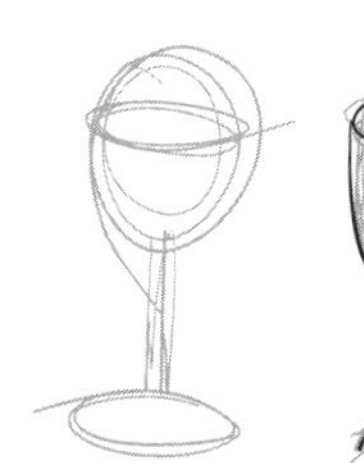

BREAK

TIP: Combine icons, text and tabs to create awesome illustrations to enhance your flip chart, create birthday invitations etc.

2.6 ARROWS & CONNECTING ELEMENTS

Arrows are a great way of connecting elements or illustrating directions and changes. Here are our favorites. Feel free to mix and match.

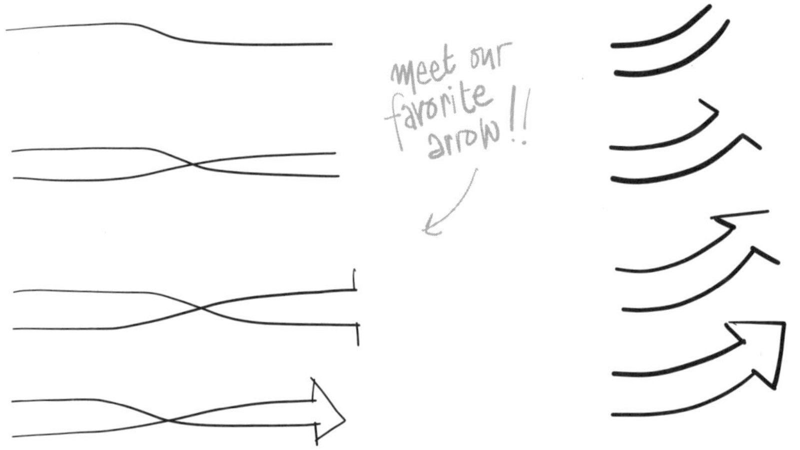

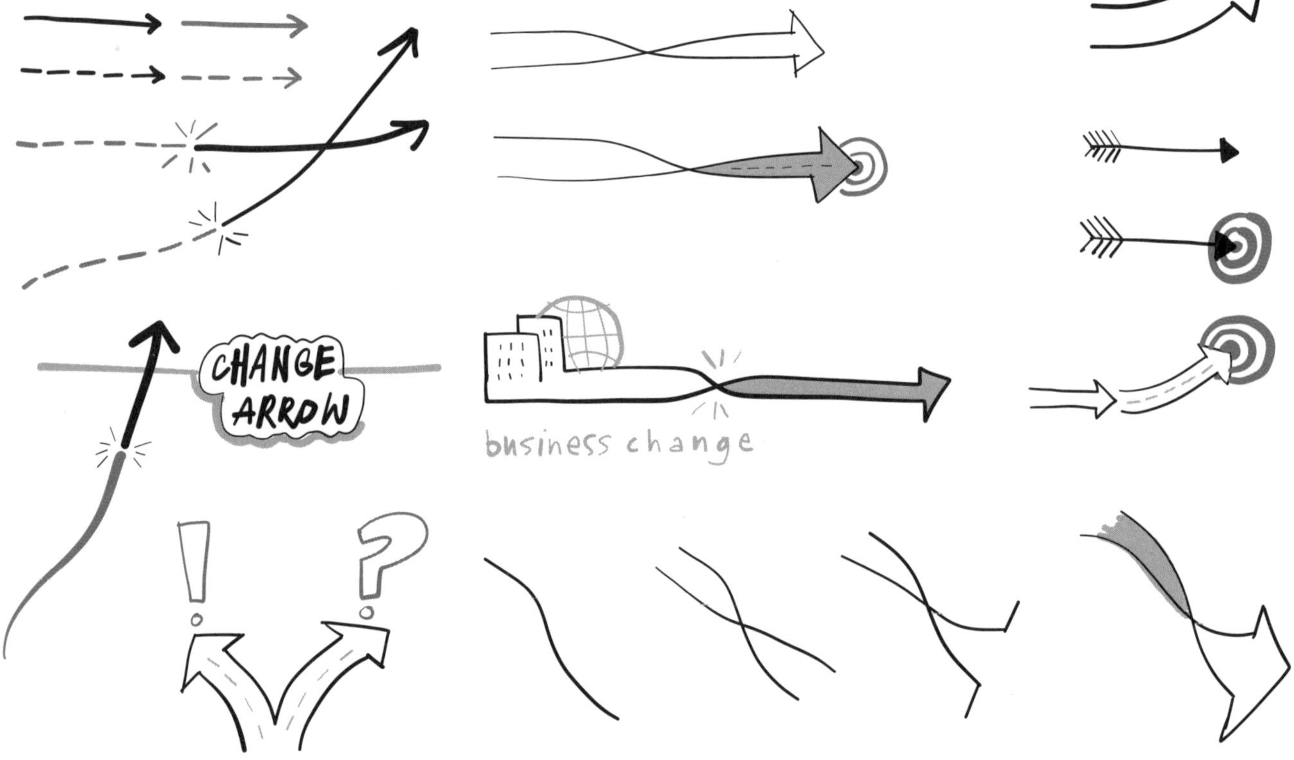

TIP: Add roadmarks, an endgoal or extra attention marks to your arrow. Also, slow down when you draw the tip of the arrow.

2.7 HEADERS AND SOME TYPOGRAPHY

This banner is a nice one to know. You can use it for titles or even create a team logo with it. This easy 'how to draw' will guide you through it.

TIP: Start by writing your title, then draw the header around it. Give your letters space and try not to work too fast.

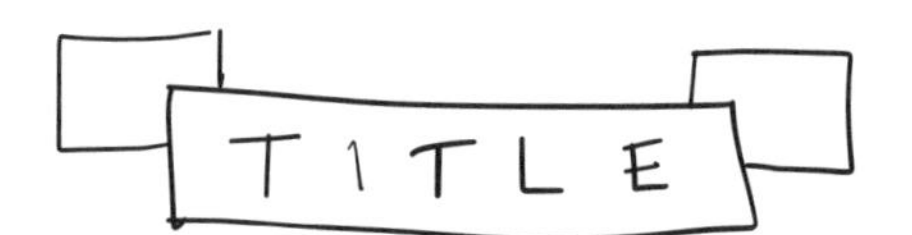

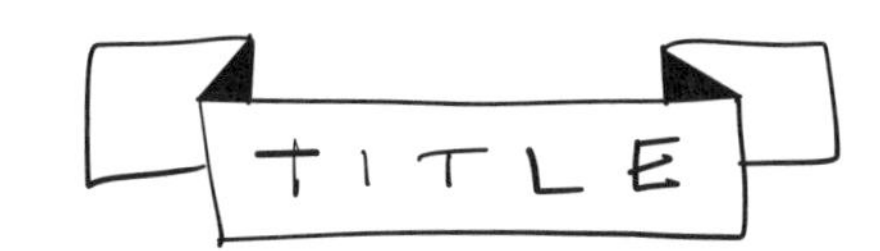

Beside your visuals, you might sometimes need some additional text. We love using different fonts. In this section are some of our favorites.

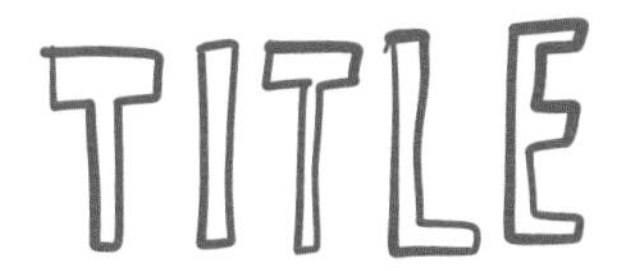

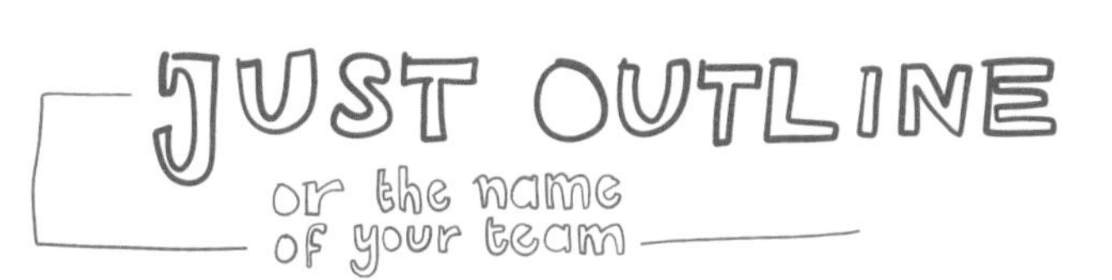

You've heard of 'word play'? With a few artistic touches you can pimp a word you're writing. Why write the word 'chaos' in clean, lean letters when you can spell it out in a chaotic font?

You might not know it, but you already have a great typographic artist in you! Remember the classic handwriting you learned at school? Dig it up and use it again.

"my handwriting which I learned at school"

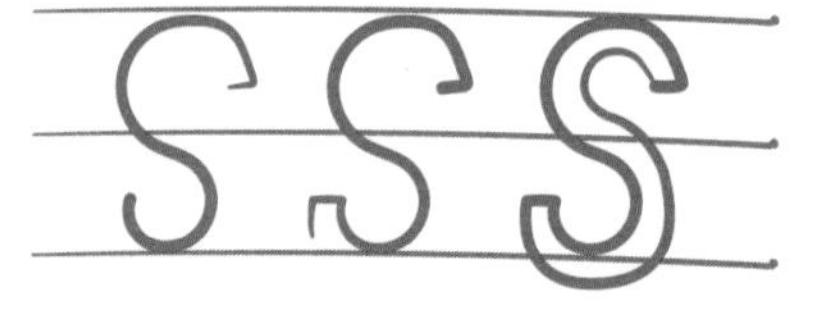

TIP: Don't draw inner shapes for a nice stencil look.

OUTLINE

TIP: Draw the 'S' using our step-by-step guide. Start with a big circle at the top and a smaller one at the bottom. Then finish up the outline.

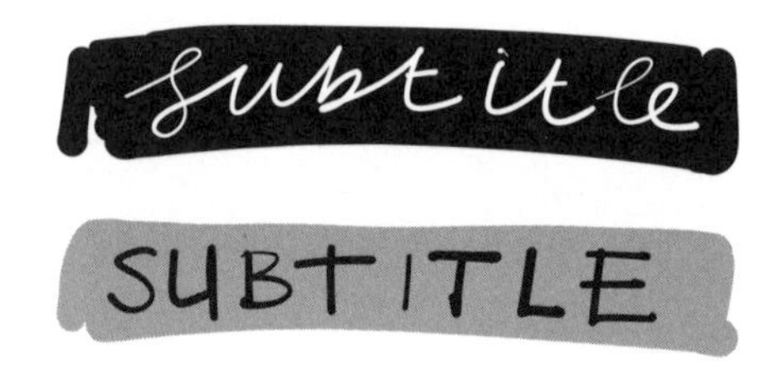

TIP: Make a black shape and write in white!

Try experimenting with wordplay by combining words with images. Use icons, different fonts, word clouds, arrows and try out different background colors.

2.8 TABS; HOW TO PIMP YOUR VISUAL STORY

If you frequently use flip charts, you can liven them up simply by drawing a tab. This is a big square on your flip topped by an icon or text block. Fill in with sticky notes, processes, arrows or text if needed.

TIP: Draw an outline around your title and provide it with a shadow.

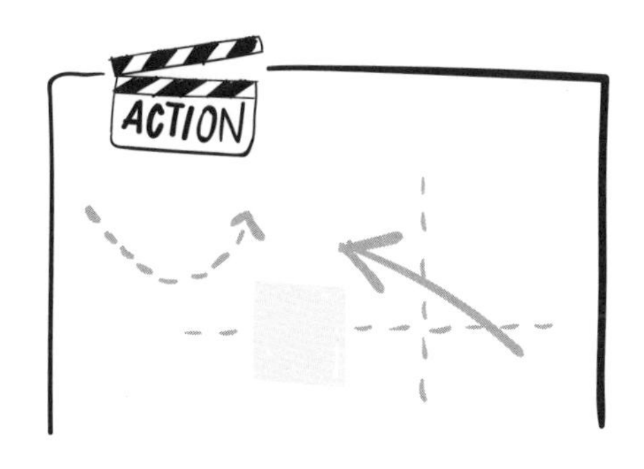

If you want to make a grid in your tab and/or use arrows, make them grey. This will make sure the connecting elements won't have the same level of attention as the most valuable information on your flip.

Google Images is your friend

2.9 BASIC ICONS & METAPHORS

Drawing doesn't have to be hard. Drawing a compass may sound difficult, but if you follow our steps you will see that it is quite simple. Always try to break down your visuals to basic shapes and then put them back together. Take inspiration from these pages and feel free to copy. By copying, you store the image in your visual memory.

TIP: Your icon will look even better if you use thick and thin lines.

ANGRY!
WOW
1
1
1
1
1
1
2
3
S

LAW
BREAK
a b c
√X = 4
S=R²

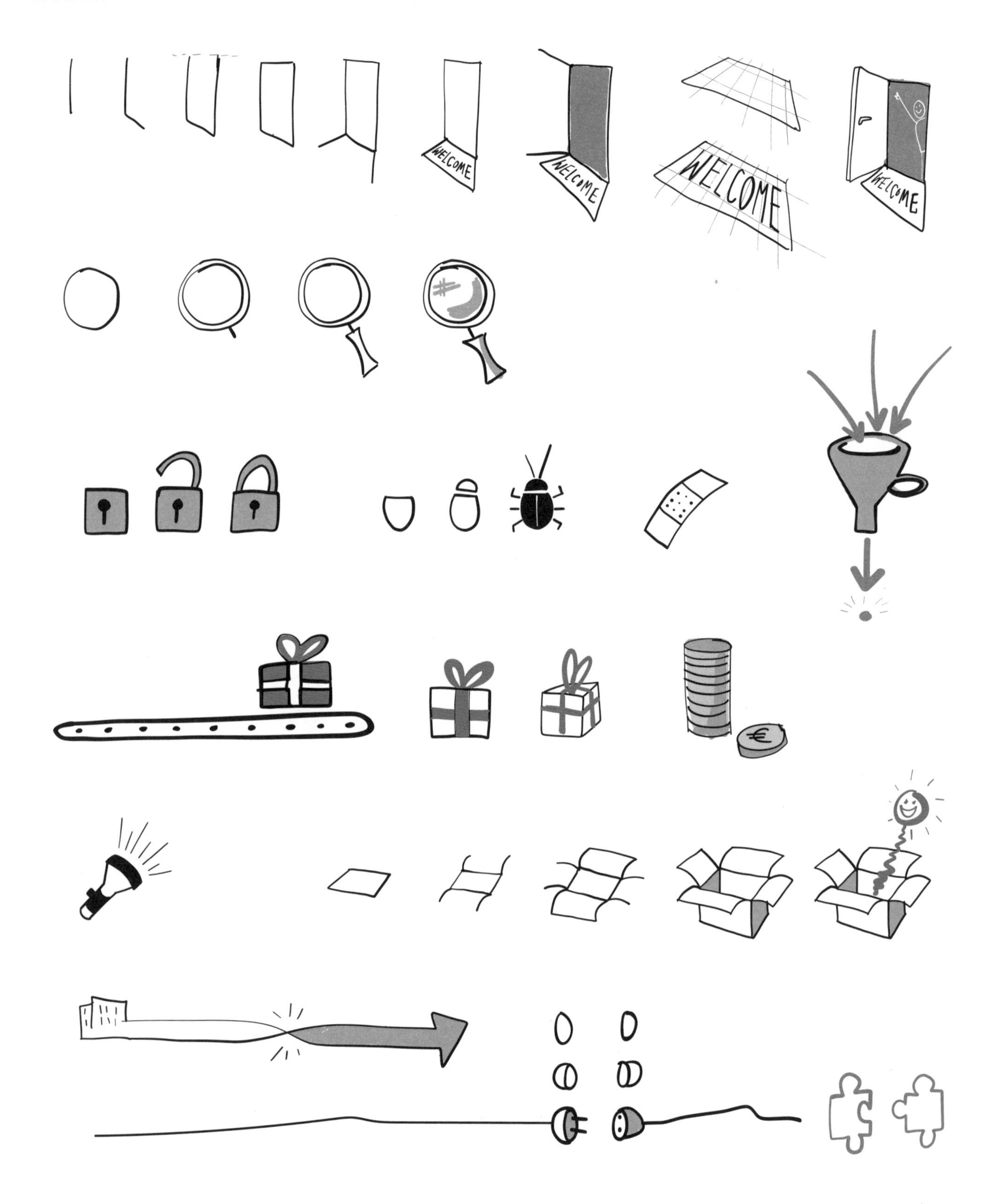
WELCOME
WELCOME
WELCOME
WELCOME

TEST
PLAN
CHECK LIST
31
31

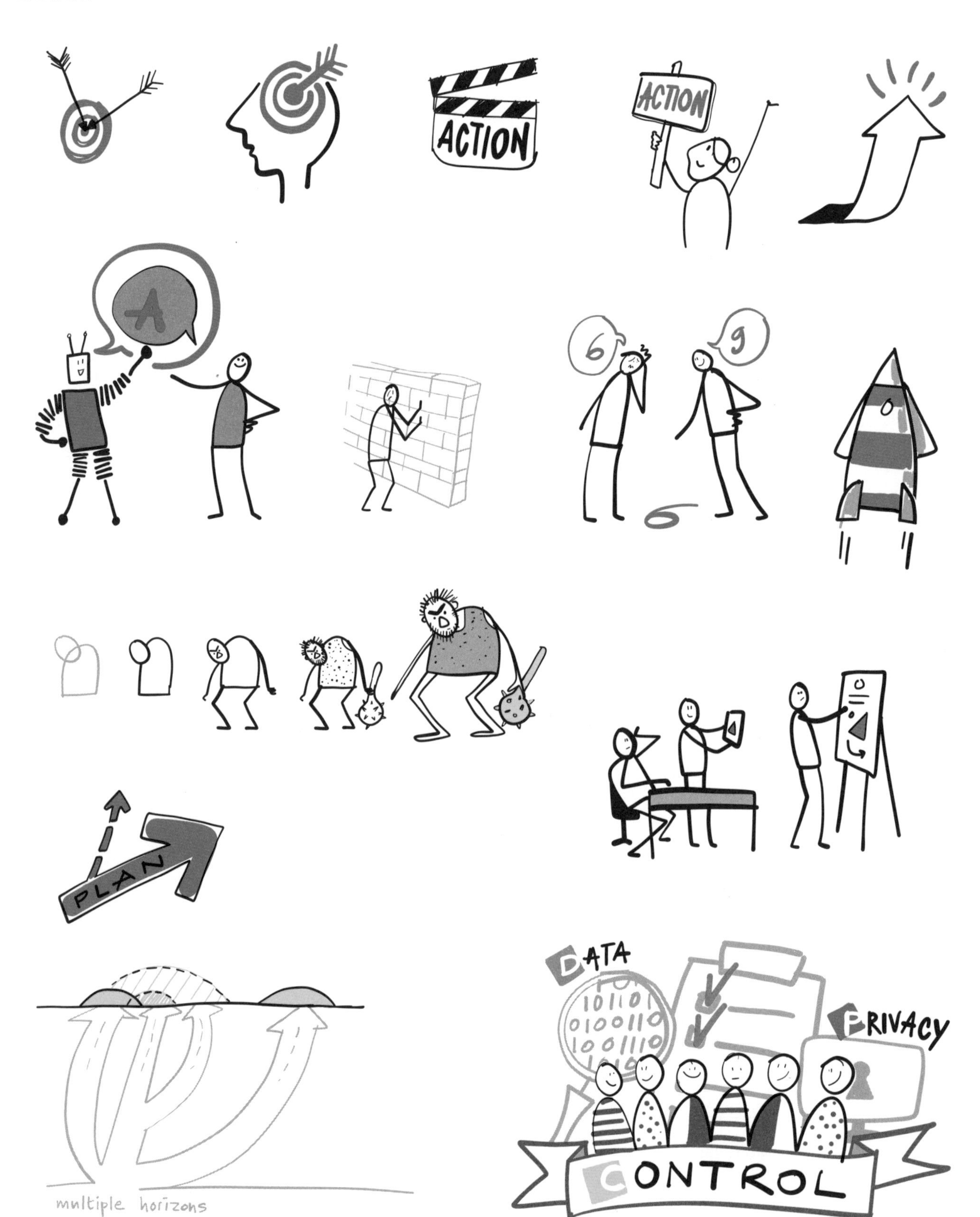
ACTION
ACTION
A
6
9
PLAN
multiple horizons
DATA
PRIVACY
CONTROL

Now you have learned some drawing basics, you can start stringing together pictures to form a visual story.

What Lifts us UP ?
WHAT KEEPS US DOWN?

3. VISUAL STORYTELLING TEMPLATING

Telling stories helps us make sense of the world. When we tell a story, we use all kinds of techniques to engage our audience: Voice intonations, facial expressions, hand gestures.
But they are not always enough to bring to life complex, abstract principles.
Sure, we can write it down, but more often than not you need a big chunk of dry text that can be hard to process.

"A picture is worth a thousand words"
We all know this old adage. It refers to the notion that a complex idea can be conveyed with just a single image.
The meaning or essence of the subject is more effectively conveyed by an image than a written or spoken description. Visual aids are powerful tools for conveying information and ideas and for enhancing your storytelling.

And it's so simple!

All you need is something to draw on. You can use a piece of paper, a tablet, a whiteboard, a flipchart or even the back of a napkin to share information and stimulate creativity.

The power of Visual Storytelling
We have to work together in an accelarating environment in which we have to process an increasing amount of information. Visuals help to highlight different perspectives, break down the information into manageable components and prioritize actions.

This chapter will teach you methods and techniques and provide some easy-to-use templates for creating your own captivating visual stories!

3.1 HEAD AND HEART

In business settings, information is mostly conveyed through written text, discussion, data and diagrams.

These more or less abstract forms of communication can be enriched with schematic drawings to grab your audience's attention in a creative way.

To successfully process the huge flow of information in today's data-driven world we need a vivid, mixed media cocktail.

We are convinced that it is not enough to simply focus on a person's head. You also have to touch their heart.

To win over the hearts and minds of your audience, you need to present information in visuals that are rich in creativity, conviction and passion.

TIP: Trust your creativity when making a visual template.

3.2 THE CREATIVE CYCLE STEP BY STEP

To create a visual story that resonates with your audience, you have to go through a certain process. Let's call it the creative cycle.

Below, we show this cycle and in the rest of this chapter we provide a practical, step-by-step guide to the process.

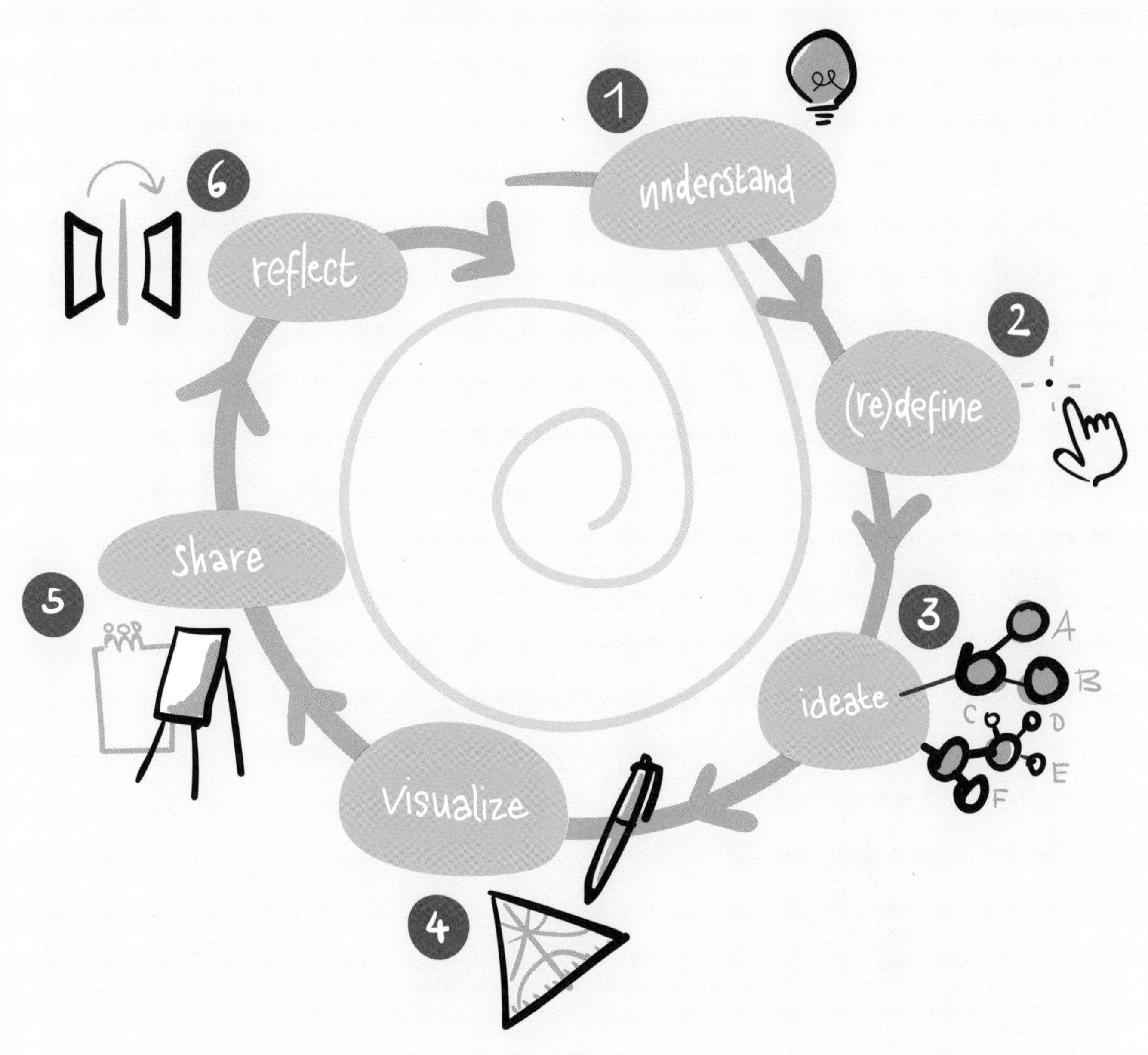

UNDERSTAND, (RE)DEFINE AND IDEATE

Understand

Define your case. Start by identifying what you want to achieve. What is the issue you would like to address? And what is the ideal situation you would like to achieve?

(Re)define the objective

Reach a deeper understanding of the story that you want to tell. Clarify on what you want to accomplish. Verify your audience and think about key messages that you want to bring across. Identify key stakeholders and partners in crime that might want to contribute to your story. Build the rationale for your story and test the water with some key influencers or experts to make sure that your story stands.

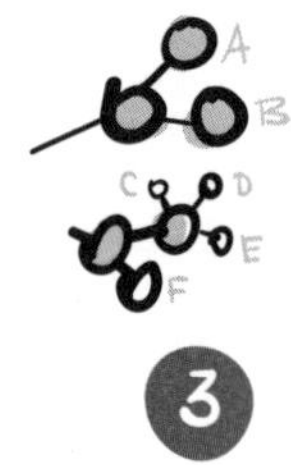

Ideate

Ideation is the creative process of generating and developing visual concepts that can support your story and your key messages. At this point it is important to capture a variety of visual concepts and take different perspectives. There are always many ways to visualize a story or build a visual that supports a key message. So make it a team effort. Depending on your audience one visual concept might resonate better than the other.

TIP: Dream up, generate, develop and communicate new ideas. Draw the ideas on cards and phrase them in just 2 or 3 words. React on each others ideas without talking, there will be plenty of time for discussion later. Don't be afraid to be silly and absurd.

At this stage, your drawing skills do not yet fully take center stage. Sketching as many visual concepts as you can is more important.

VISUALIZE

Visualize

Now you can start visualizing the storyline you prefer. Do you want to inform your audience with an engaging presentation, or do you want a different kind of impact by sparking the whole room into action? Or maybe both? The following page shows the different approaches.

visual storytelling activates your audience, gets them involved and lets them help enrich your story.

Presentation board

This is useful when you already know what you want to convey.
The information is mostly defined and you can prepare your presentation/drawings beforehand.

There is not much interaction or input from the audience, but that doesn't mean the presentation can't be dynamic, especially when you enhance your presentation with extra drawings on the spot.

Useful for presentation of (business) plans, annual figures or any kind of process within your organization. (Basically, to transfer information from you to your audience.)

You can build the visual story by creating a metaphor together! This can involve input from the group, so make it a joint effort!

TIP: A session can have more then one board. Use drawings on sticky notes to create an animated presentation.

Activation board

This is useful when you know the contours of what you want to share but can't yet predict the exact outcome. Or when you want to gather input or work out a strategy or vision.

You can discuss and share ideas and visualize them on your board(s). You can, for example, use separate boards to identify benefits and danger zones.

Sketch or draw with the group and invite them to add sticky notes. This way of communicating is great for involving everyone. It energizes your audience and makes people more committed both during and after the meeting.

Can be deployed for strategy meetings, discussing customer journeys, problem solving.

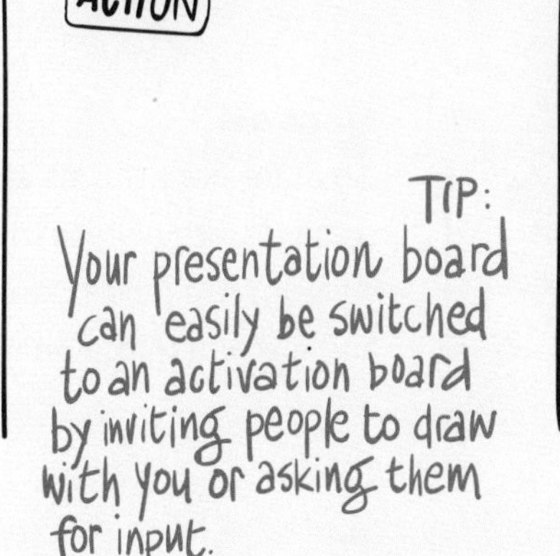

TIP:
Your presentation board can easily be switched to an activation board by inviting people to draw with you or asking them for input.

Choose your plan

When you tell a story, you often use body language to establish direction and order. Below, we translate these gestures and guides into visual plans and design templates.

which way do your arms or body automatically MOVE while telling your story?
KEEP THIS IN MIND WHEN CHOOSING A DESIGN PLAN!

The list

When your story goes from top to bottom. Great for listings suchs as agendas, programs and timetables.

Steps

When your story starts at the bottom and goes up. Useful for roadmaps going all the way up to the horizon, also great for calculations.

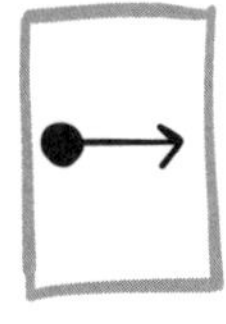

The Timeline

Used to show chronological steps (a-to-z), timelines (also different levels of timelines in one design), desirable situations and changes.

The Road

An evergreen. Frequently used for drawing customer journeys, steps to take, milestones to reach and possible opportunities and dangers on the way to the dot on the horizon.

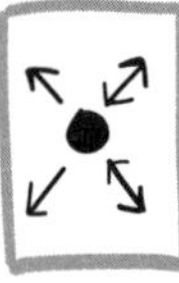

Mandala

Great for brainstorms and interactive sessions with no restricted outcome. Inviting for people to put sticky notes and mix and match on the board.

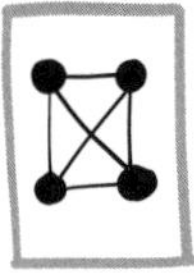

The Matrix

Handy for showing different types of information about one subject such as a SWOT analysis. Also ideal for showing do's and don'ts on one board.

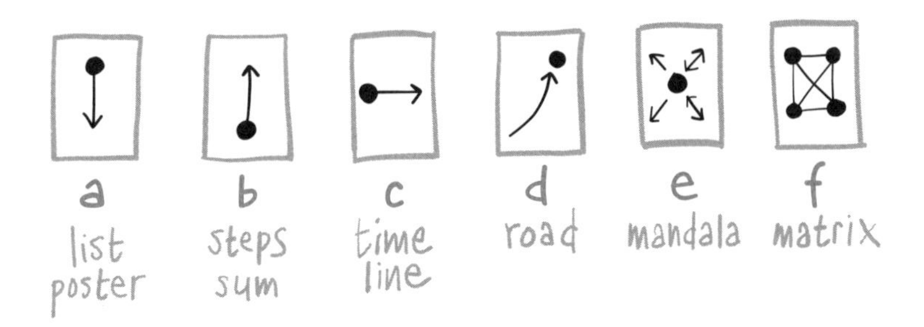

Choose a metaphor and make your design

Once you have picked a plan, you can start sketching. Then choose a metaphor that fits your situation and you can start making your design.

You have plenty of options. If you are drawing a journey, you can use the road template, but should it go towards the sunset or wind its way through mountains? What can you add to the visual and what can you leave out?

You can use one of our examples or pick one of your own – use your imagination!

Note that a story can contain multiple plans or templates. For example, start with a mandala where you collect information about your current situation, then use those insights to draw up a road where you show you plan of improvement.

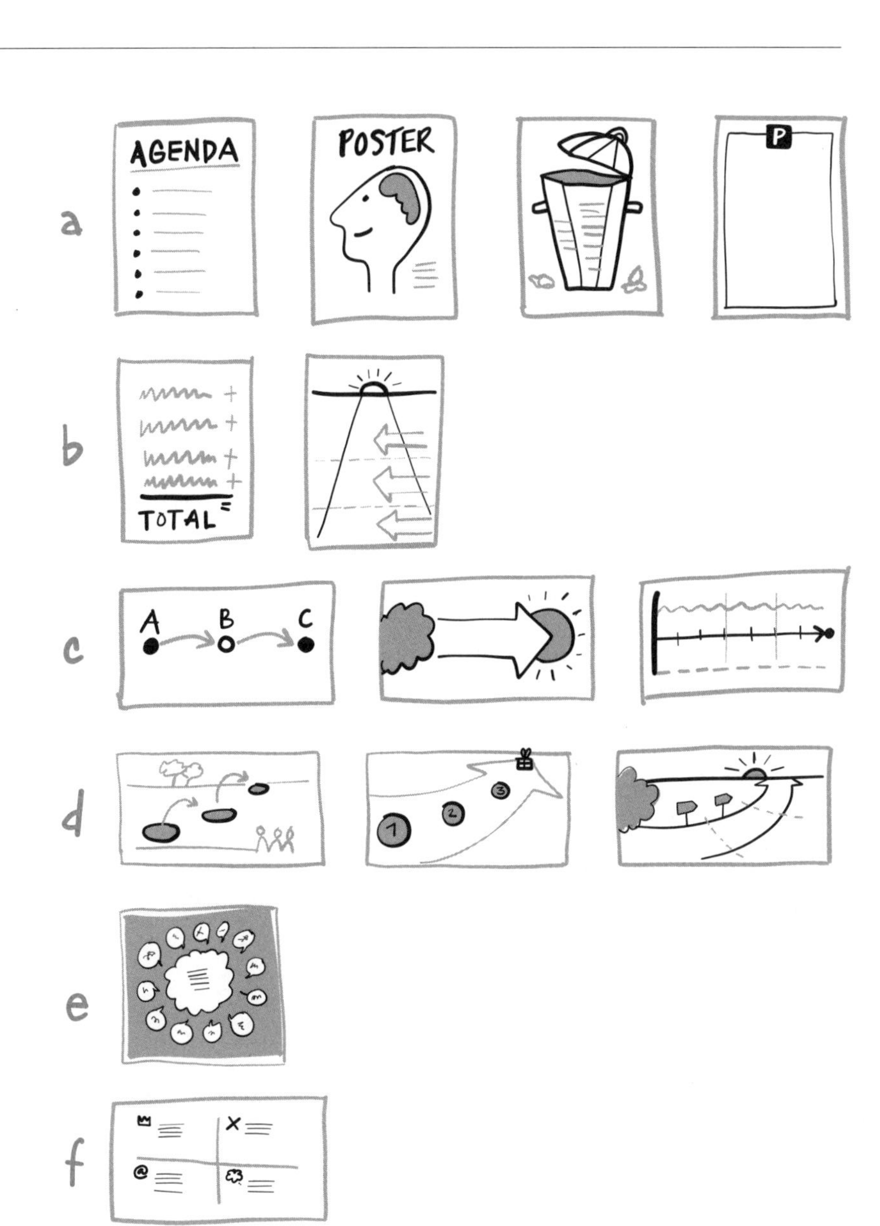

Are you struggling to find a metaphor?

Here is how to get unstuck:

build, draw, construct together on this metaphor

Acknowledge it!
This is important! If it feels wrong, it is wrong. Stop, re-think and start over.

Co-create
Ask colleagues or the group for input. Ask them "How can I best draw..."? or "What should I add here"? You will receive a flood of ideas and enthusiasm.

Sketch and talk
As someone throws out an idea, quickly encourage the others to sketch out what it might look like. As you discuss a case or problem, listen carefully! People often talk in metaphors. Ask additional questions if necessary. Try explaining an issue as you would to a 5-year-old.

Look around!
What does it resemble?
Could you use a sport as a metaphor for a journey or perhaps a movie star as a fictive client.
Take your inspiration from nature. Mountains, rivers, trees! What do they represent? What characteristics do they have?

Play with cliché
Be playful and inspired to get more ideas. Use clichés because these resonate very clearly. Examples:

"when a door shuts, another opens."

"Money doesn't grow on trees"

"follow the river and you will reach the sea"

"Don't make a mountain out of a molehill"

"Tip of the iceberg"

TIP: Not all the ideas you generate will suit your circumstances. Save them! They might be useful another time.

TIP: Explore the ideas that seem viable. See what could be added, combined or maybe left out?
Once you have found your metaphor, all you have to figure out is how to draw it!

SHARE AND REFLECT

Share
The advantage of visual storytelling is that you keep everyone interested and focused. But more importantly it reveals hidden sentiments, assumptions and ideas. And because all the information is clearly presented, it will help your audience to point things out and provide feedback.

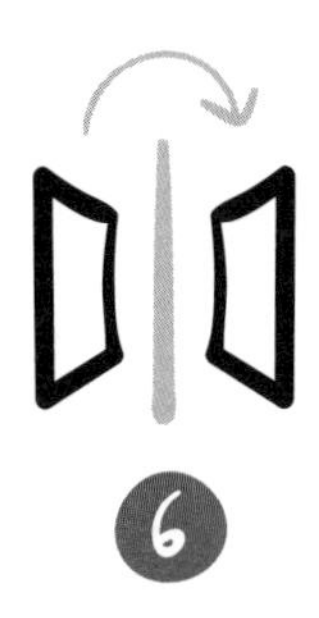

Reflect
There is always room for improvement. Ask yourself: did we miss anything? Did we do too much? What can we do without? It's also helpful to ask others for critical feedback.
This can focus on the content, or the visualization or maybe your presenting skills. Whatever it is, keep an open mind. Perhaps you will stumble upon a blind spot.

Reflect and Improve; your visual story often has multiple iterations.

If so, go back to STEP 1 of the creative cycle.

1 understand
2 (re)define
3 ideate
4 visualize
5 share
6 reflect

TIP: Take a photo of your visual so you can easily share it across different (social media) platforms.

3.3 METAPHOR TEMPLATES

Below you will find some templates which are ready-to-use or can serve as inspiration.
Don't be afraid to make the most of your chosen metaphor; include images that fit: apples, a chainsaw, roadblocks, polar bears or magnifying glasses.

WEATHER FORECAST

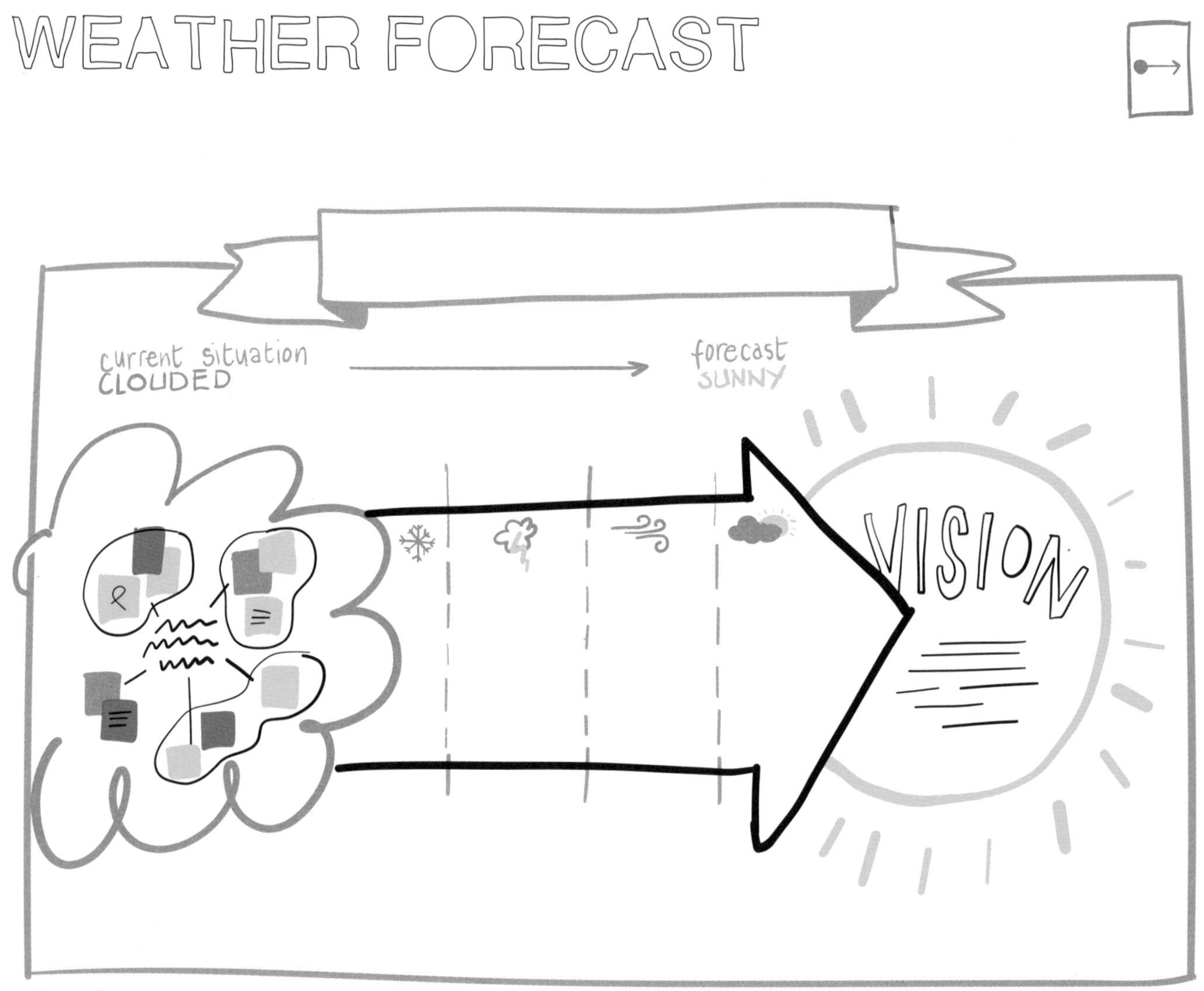

BASED ON 'GRAPHIC GAMEPLAN' BY DAVID SIBBET

Looking for a visual vocabulary to build up your story? Here are some examples, but remember that there will also be good visual thinkers in the group who can help generate metaphors and ideas.

ICEBERG

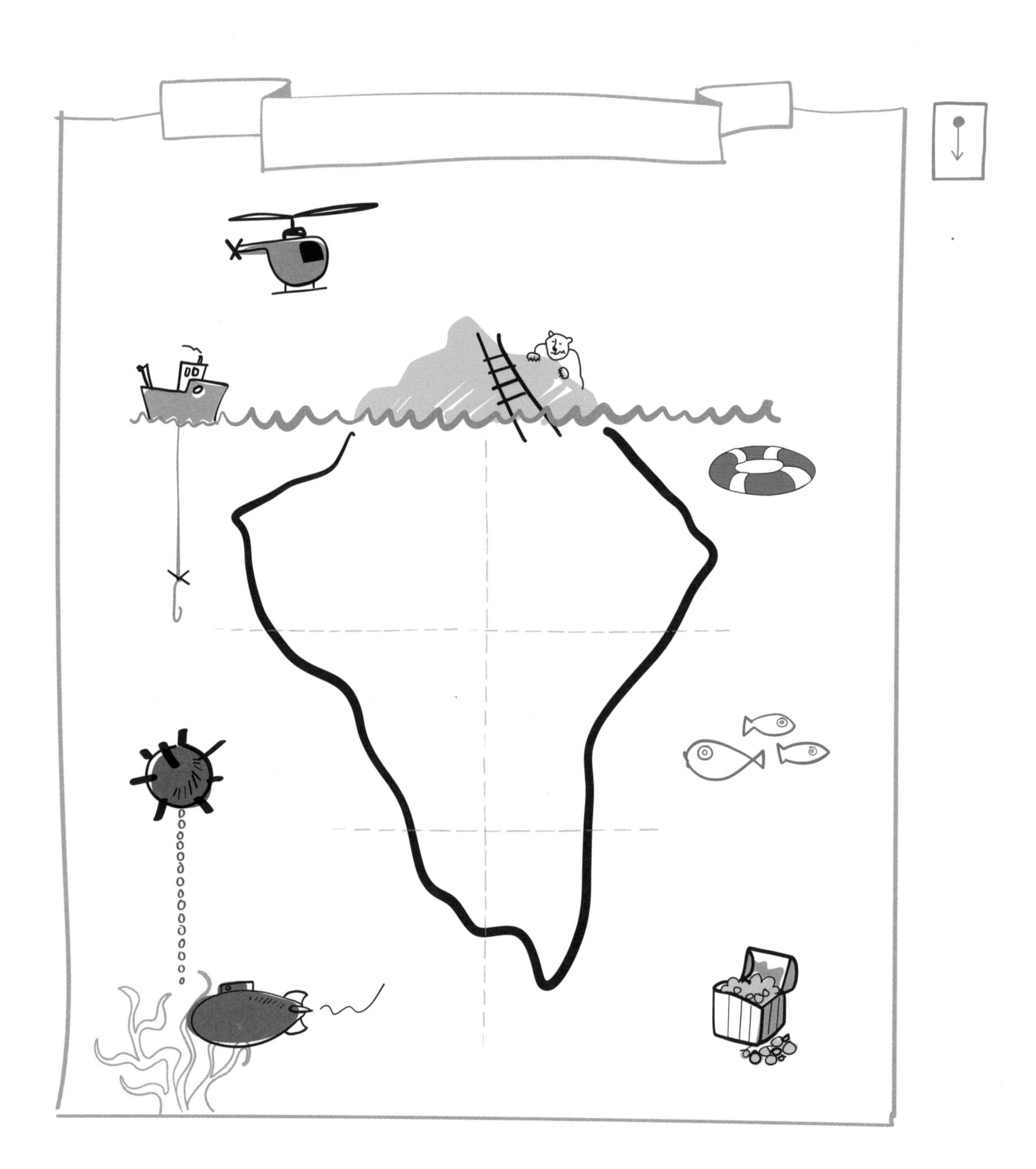

action templates:
use sticky notes-input to collect information

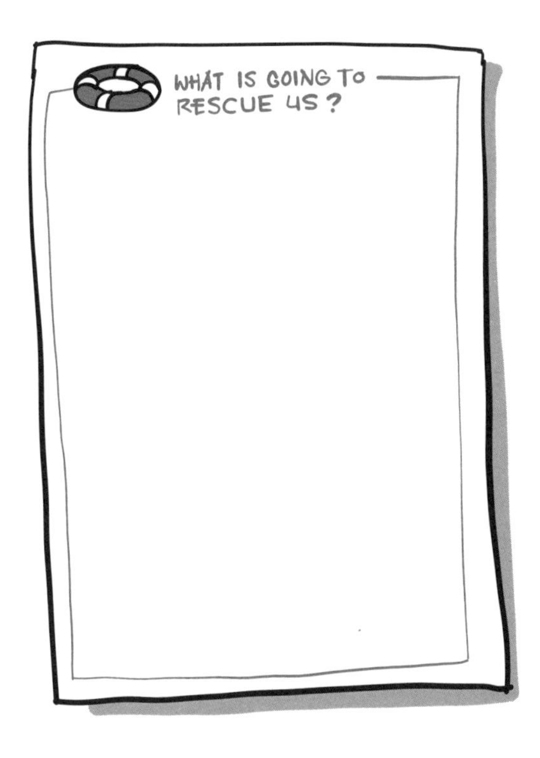
WHAT IS GOING TO RESCUE US?

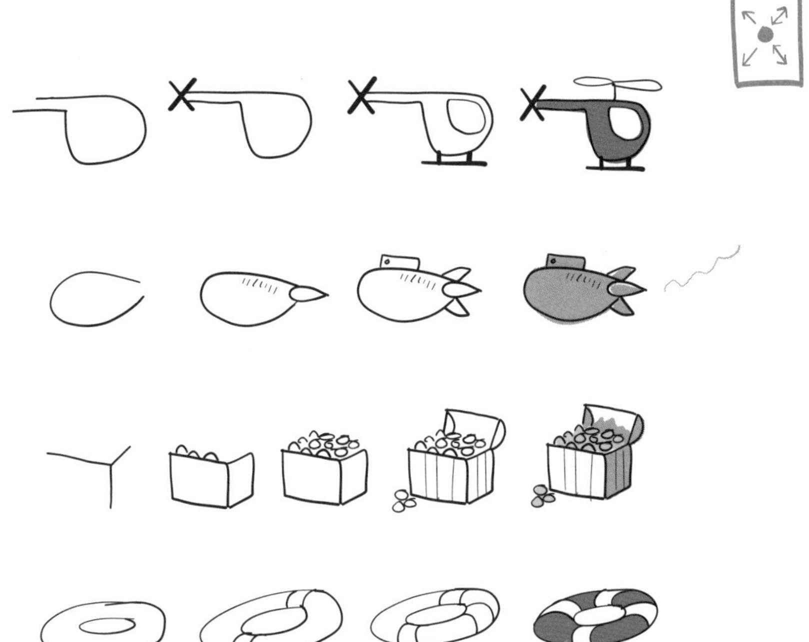

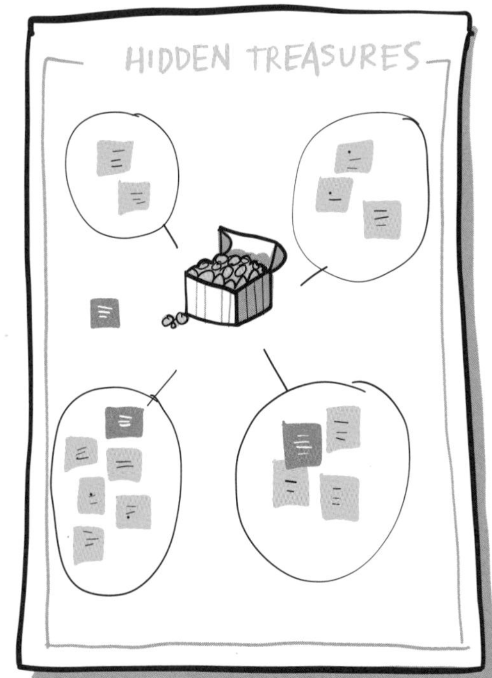
HIDDEN TREASURES

ROADMAP

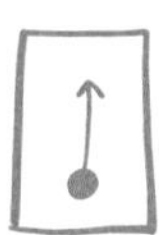

FINISH
(multiple horizons)
!
?
short cut
FINISH
A
C
B

HARRY POTTER

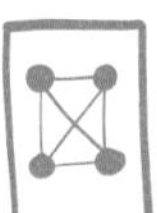

Think outside the box! Why not use a famous book (character) or movie and make it fun! Use a famous scene or theme from a series or movie like Harry Potter. How cool would it be to make a Lord of the Rings template showing all the possible pitfalls and opportunities you will encounter on your journey?

STEPPING STONES

action templates

POSTERS

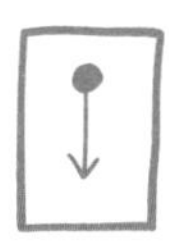

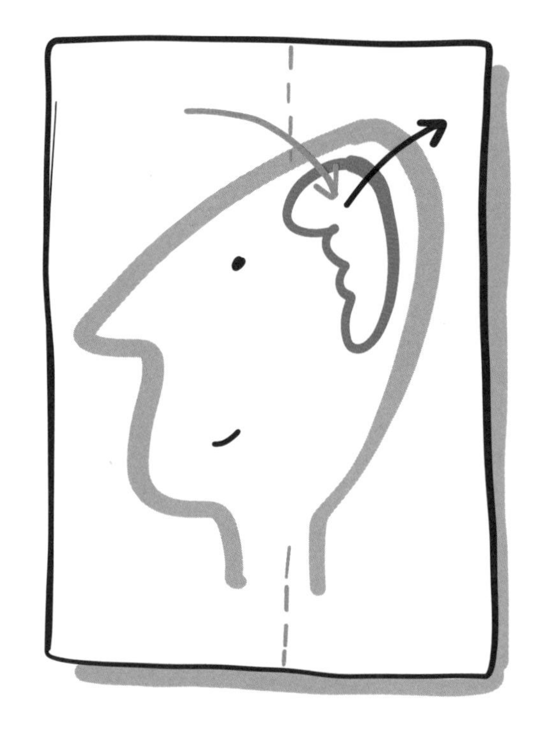

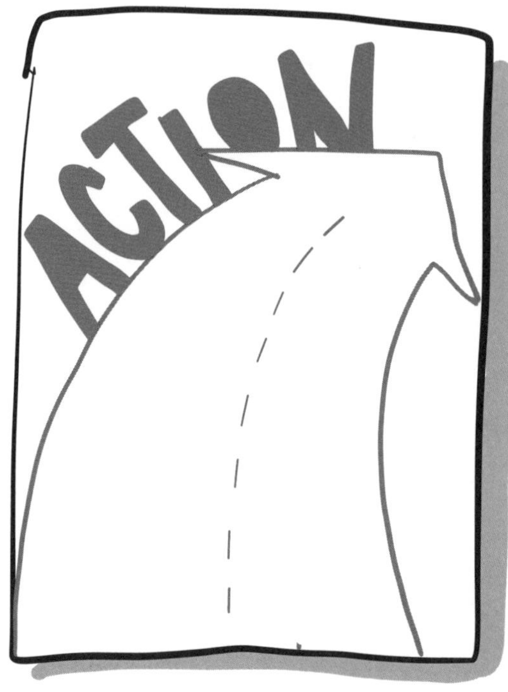

TIP: If the group gets side-tracked, just write whatever you are discussing on a parking board and get back on topic (while promising to return to the parking board at the end of the meeting).

BROWN PAPER WALL

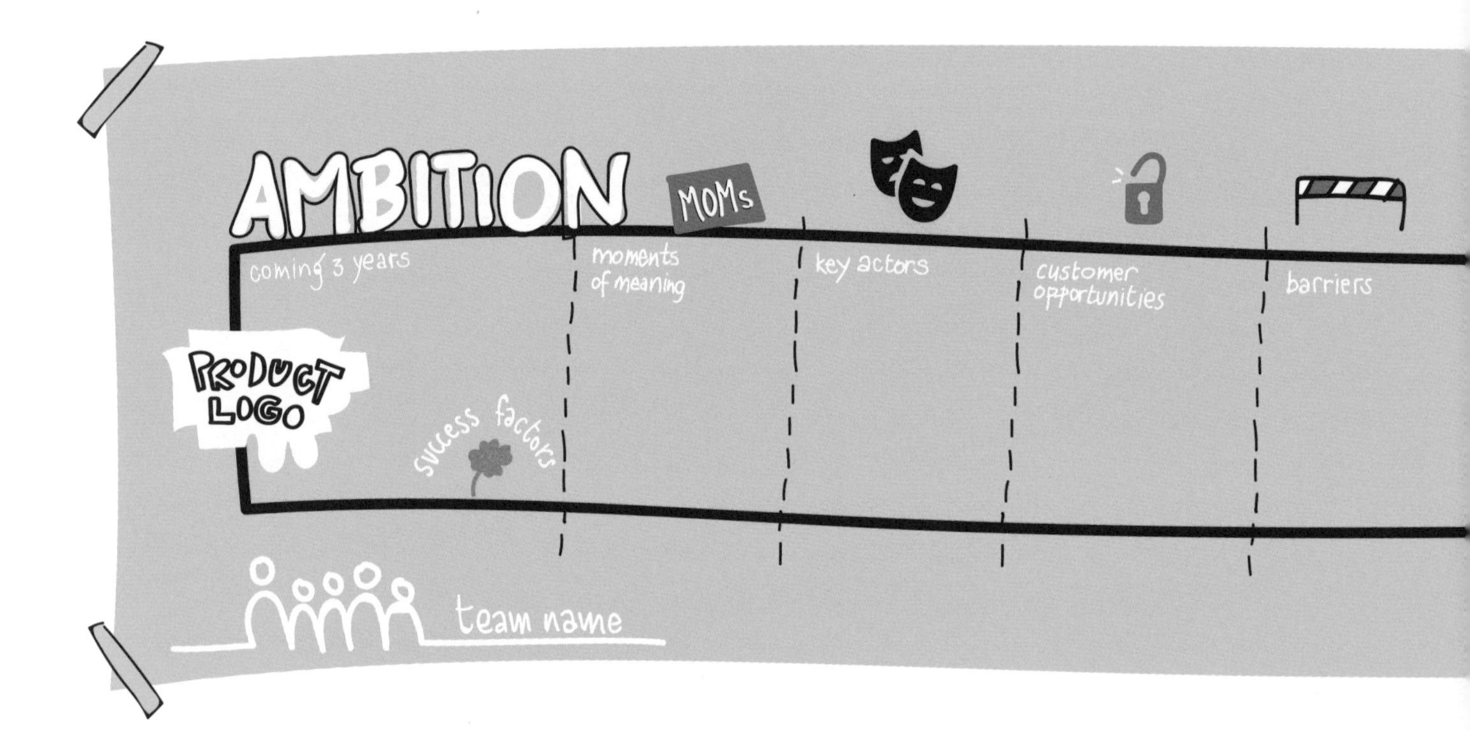

SUCCESS FACTORS
→
→
→
→
→

START with your success factors (to point out the current situation)

TIP: To start off stick a long strip of brown paper to a wall – at least 10 meters!

TIP: Use a small piece of the paper to check the effect of your black and gray markers. Use a white marker for extra impact – white on brown has a very cool effect.

A brown paper wall is useful for making your sales, product or business plan or to map any kind of process within your organization. Often it is used to clearify and tune your (long term) strategy or vision. It contains so many different facets that it is best to have multiple sessions to fill the wall.

You could even make it a three or four day event!

STRATEGIC WALL
product journey

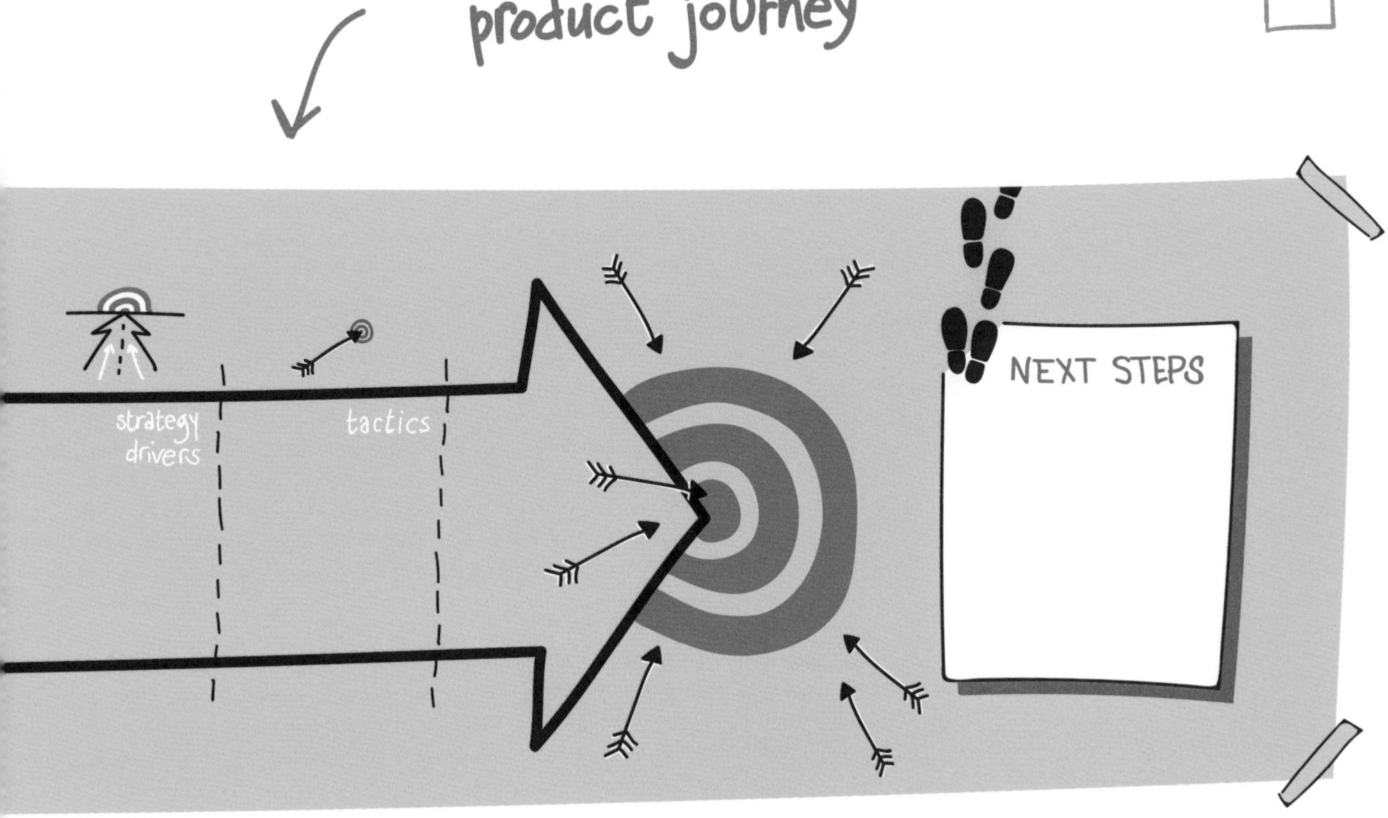

strategy drivers

tactics

NEXT STEPS

Set up the template and then gradually fill it in. Parts of this template can be worked out separately: in groups or in another room.

Keep going back to the strategic wall so you can keep track of the big picture and have presentations every now and then to inform each other of findings and insights.

During the meetings have everybody contribute by drawing on sticky notes. This generates discussion and helps align people's ideas.
In the final session, fill in all the areas, summarize and draw conclusions.

As you can see, the brown paper wall is a great way of using visual communication to enhance business meetings. In chapter 4, we show you 9 concrete examples of how to embed drawing in your business.

TIP: It's a good idea to add a sheet at the end where you can write down NEXT STEPS or ACTIONS. This brings into focus what needs to be done immediately or in the near future.

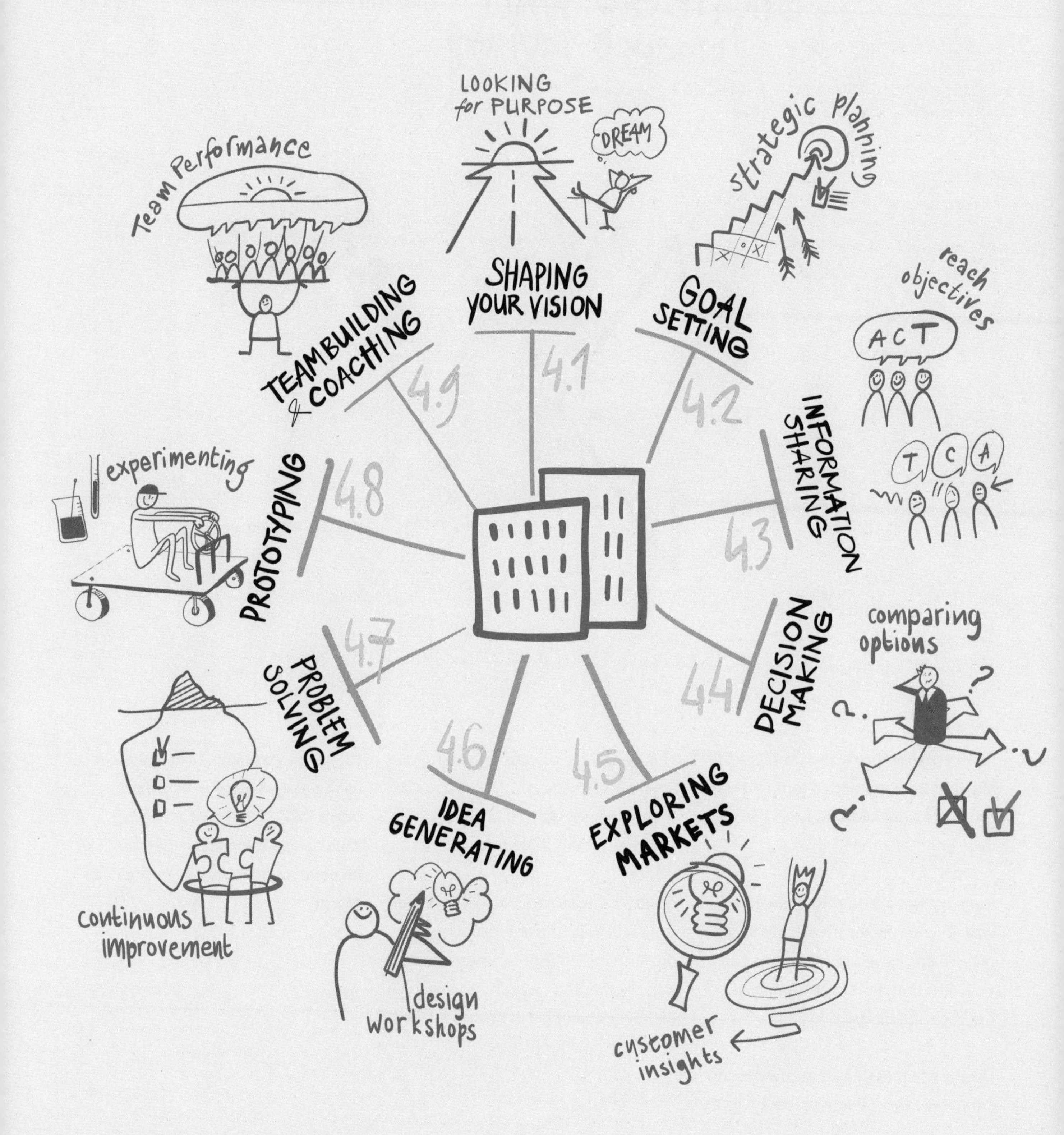
LOOKING
for PURPOSE
DREAM
Team Performance
strategic planning
SHAPING
YOUR VISION
GOAL
SETTING
TEAMBUILDING
& COACHING
reach
objectives
ACT
4.9
4.1
4.2
INFORMATION
SHARING
TCA
experimenting
PROTOTYPING
4.8
4.3
4.7
PROBLEM
SOLVING
DECISION
MAKING
4.4
comparing
options
4.6
4.5
IDEA
GENERATING
EXPLORING
MARKETS
continuous
improvement
design
workshops
customer
insights

4. VISUAL THINKING IN BUSINESS SETTINGS

Facts, figures, plans, methods, budgets and deadlines often dominate today's work environment. Whether you work in technology, financial services, the public sector, health care or manufacturing, visual thinking will help you and your colleagues to be more effective.

It is also not unusual that you look back on projects and realize that you forgot to make time to take a step back and look at the bigger picture.

In this chapter we introduce nine generic business settings in which people work in teams to realize a specific goal. Visual thinking and collaboration techniques can help you achieve goals better and faster by unlocking the "whole brain function" of workers within these settings. We provide a few hands-on good practice techniques for each setting.

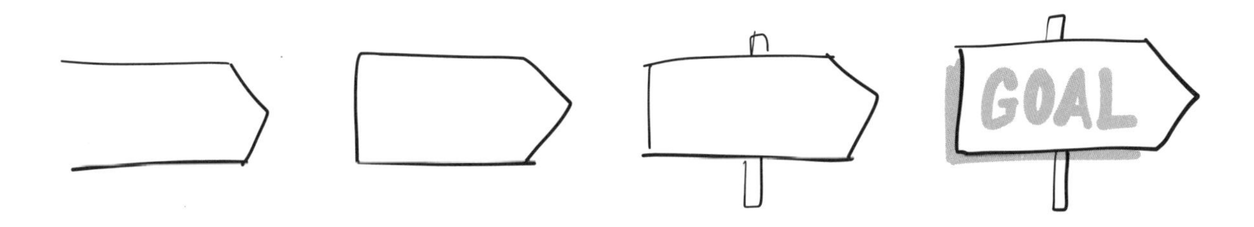

4.1 SHAPING YOUR VISION
LOOKING FOR PURPOSE

Clarity of purpose and vision is the first step in goal setting. Most companies have vision statements that summarize their view of the future. A fun exercise is to look at vision statements and try to guess which companies they come from.
For example, Wikipedia wants us to "Imagine a world in which every single person is given free access to the sum of all human knowledge." Less inspiring vision statements simply state a company's goal to "be the number one (industry/product) in the world" or "provide world-class (service/ product)". They may inspire you, but do such generic statements give you enough direction?
It's hard to boil down a vision into just a few words. Visual techniques can clarify and capture your vision in an inspiring and comprehensive way.

YOU WILL LEARN:

> **Visual Collaboration Techniques**
Purpose finding
Vision boards
The golden circle – why, how, what
The heart and head exam

SETTING THE SCENE

WHO typically attends a vision workshop?

- The organization's purpose and vision are the management's responsibility, so they are generally the key stakeholders. But their purpose and vision need to be shared and institutionalized throughout the entire organization.
- Not only top management develops a vision. At lower levels, for specific functional areas and layers in the organization, people need to have a vision of the future direction.
- Sometimes you have a visionary and charismatic leader who builds and spreads the vision. But often you see that management needs inspiration and dialogue to bring clarity to their purpose and vision for the future.
- Management can ask members of the organization to come up with their own ideas on the future of the company. In this way, they maximize the available talent and insights.
- The organization's strategy department and external strategy consultants are typically involved as advisers during the formulation of the vision.

WHEN and where do organizations (re)create their vision?

- A vision and related strategy need to be dynamic in this rapidly changing world. Companies can't afford to set down a vision for the coming 10 years that cannot be adjusted during its enactment.
- However, organizations generally set their vision and strategy every 3-5 years and have annual reviews.
- It is important that corporate visions are aligned with the visions of the different functional areas and layers of your organization.
- If you have an agile organization, each squad's purpose needs to be aligned with the corporate purpose and vision.
- Typically the organization's purpose and vision is (re)created during a so-called "off-site", which basically means that everyone involved steps out of their daily environment and gathers at an external location.

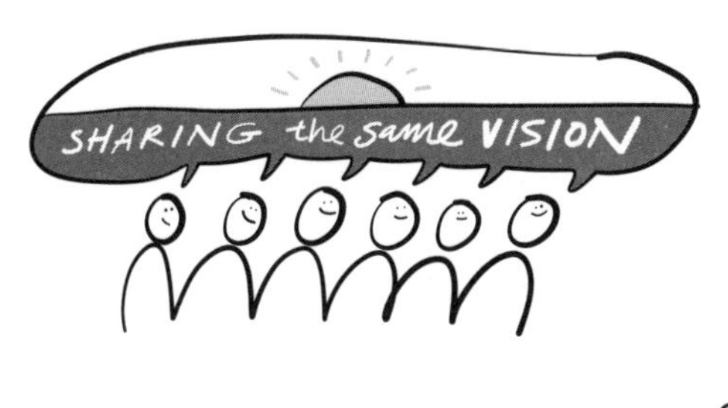

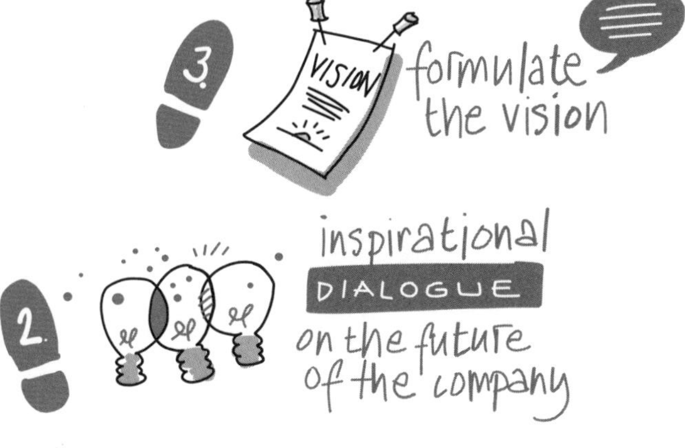

WHAT happens during the process of creating a vision?

- Shaping a vision is about dreaming the future. There are various ways to orchestrate a process to create a vision. The one you use depends on the state of the company and the needs of management.
- In general, there are three steps: the first is gathering and analyzing trends, the second is to have an inspirational dialogue to share and synthesize ideas on the future of the company. The third is to formulate the vision.
- As part of the process, some management teams go on inspirational trips to for instance Silicon Valley and visit successful organizations to learn before they (re)set their own vision for the coming years.

VISUAL COLLABORATION TECHNIQUES

Imagine that you are part of a team that is responsible for organizing an offsite to shape your company's purpose and vision. You believe the current vision is too generic and does not provide enough direction and inspiration for the organization to take ownership and action. Therefore, your ambition is to do it differently and shape a vision that is purpose-driven, clear, inspirational and provides direction about the company's future. How would you use the time during the offsite to achieve your ambition?
Below you can find four of our preferred visual techniques that could help you and your team.

PURPOSE FINDING

Understanding the reason your organization exists helps you to inspire people with purpose-driven change rather than a pursuit of profit or cost cutting. Your purpose provides strategic clarity, helps drive x-functional innovation, creates brand value and is a critical factor for your organization in retaining talent. However, defining your organization's purpose can be difficult. Open sessions can lead to long, unstructured discussions or a rational short cut that does not truly answer the fundamental "why?" question underpinning your business.
A simple model can help you find your purpose by answering four questions:

1. What do you love?
2. What does the world need?
3. What do you do well?
4. What can you be paid for?

The purpose of you or your organization can be found where your answers to all four questions meet.

TIP:

Work out the 4 different Questions in separate but corresponding colors.

Write the most important words at the intersections of the different bubbles.

Brainstorm to reach the ultimate purpose.

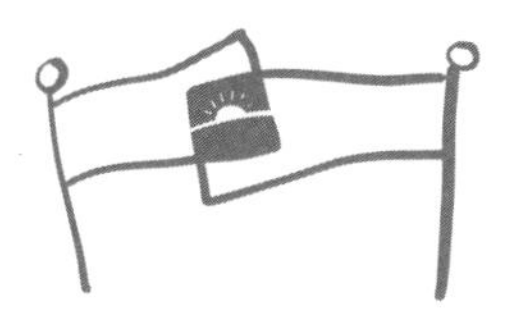

TIP: Please be aware that a purpose is multidimensional and needs input from a cross-functional team and ownership at top management level. It is also relevant to involve different regions and countries within your organization, as employees from various cultures may have very different beliefs around topics like purpose and values.

VISION BOARDS

- A vision board is a visualization or drawing of your goals as if you have already achieved them.
- When you create your vision board, seek images to represent the details of your vision and goals. In this way vision boards help clarify and sharpen your focus.
- To structure your vision board you can use your vision statement and break it down into its related key words/themes supported by images. The vision statement can be visualized through a metaphor. Alternatively, you can imagine your vision of the future by visualizing what it looks like to stakeholders like your customers, employees and investors.
- When the board is ready, the idea is that you put it somewhere clearly visible so that it reminds you of your intentions throughout the day. Invite people to contribute to the vision by, for example, adding new post-its or images.

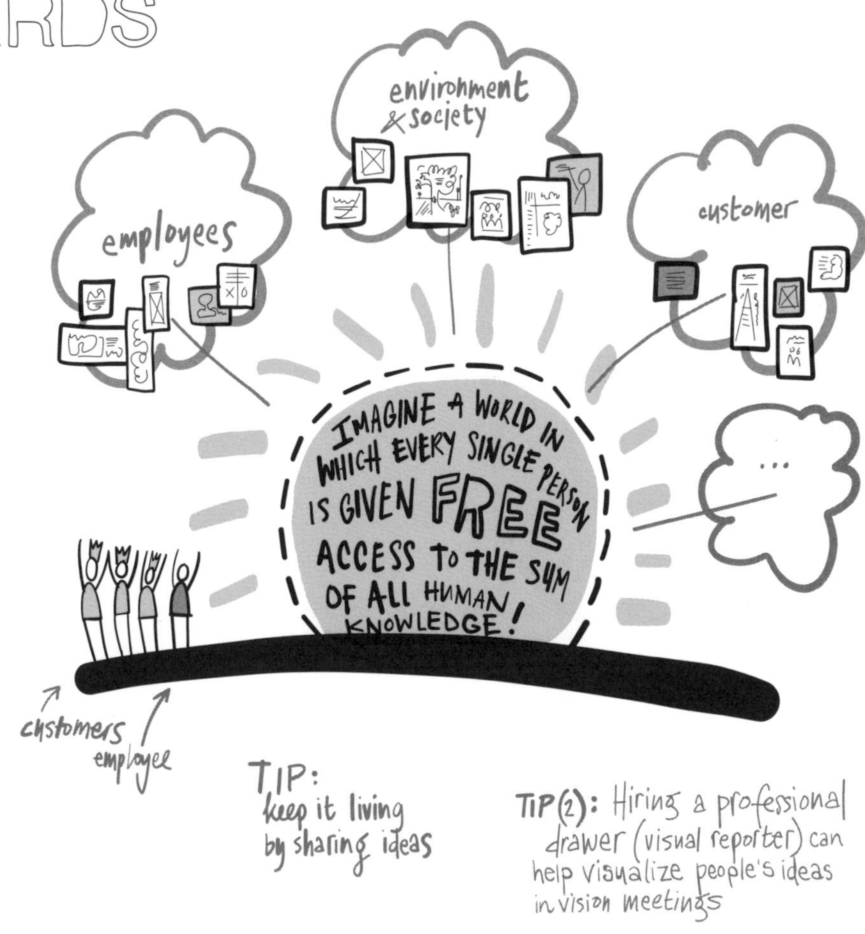

A WORLD WITH FREE ACCESS to all human knowledge
TIP: combine your vision statement in a header visual

THE GOLDEN CIRCLE: WHY, HOW, WHAT

- The golden circle – created by Simon Sinek – is a simple model that assumes three levels on which organizations and people operate: what you do, how you do it and why you do it.
- The idea behind the golden circle is that while all companies know what they do, only a few know why they do it.
- Successful organizations and people communicate inside out. They start by explaining why they do what they do, what their purpose is. In this way they are able to inspire people to take action.
- The model is a simple way to structure the purpose of your company into a compelling story.

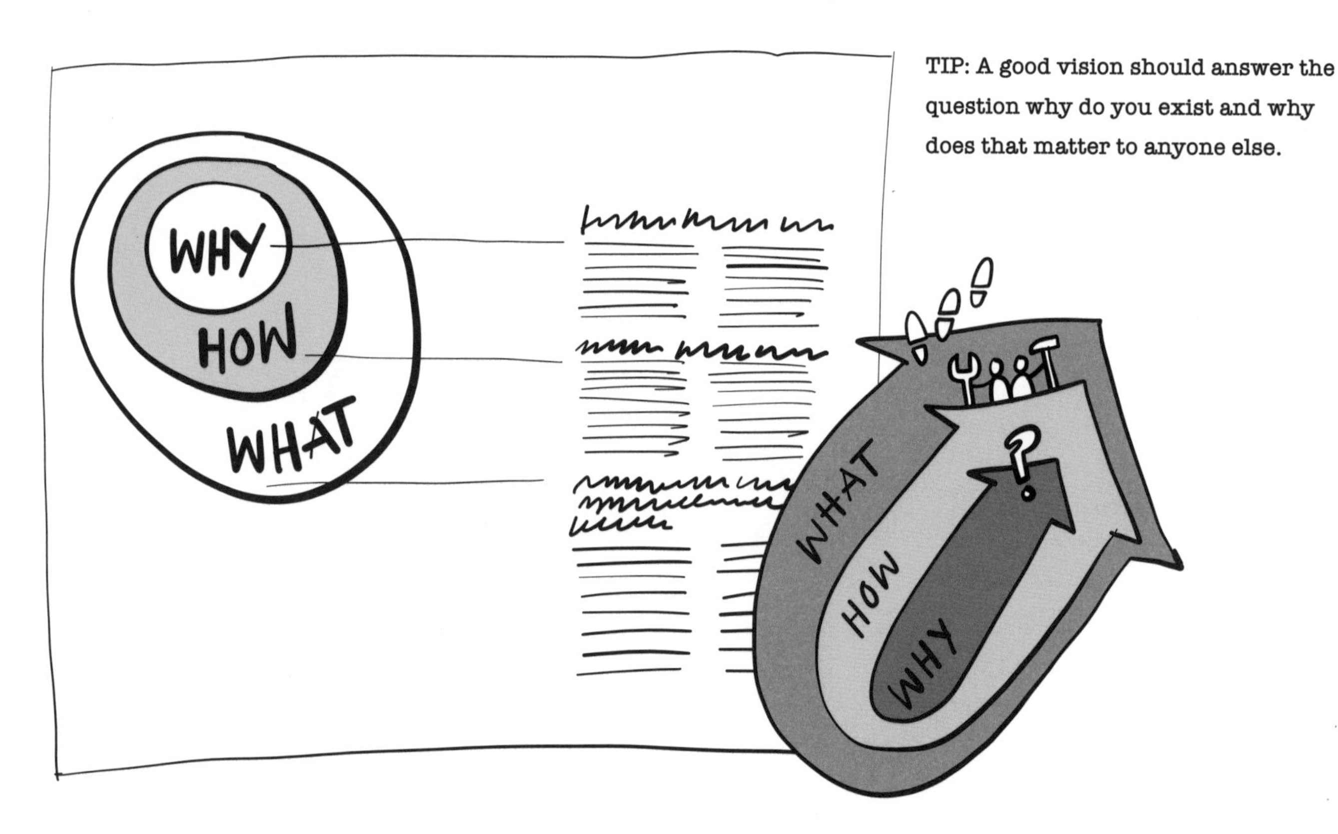

TIP: A good vision should answer the question why do you exist and why does that matter to anyone else.

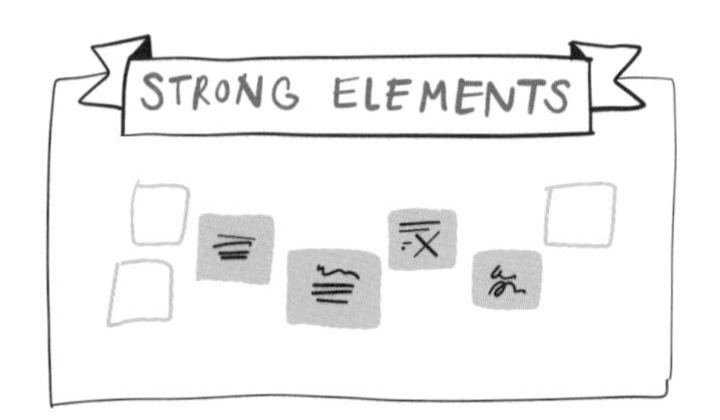

TIP: Cluster your strong elements and need-to-improve items on a new action board.

THE HEART AND HEAD TEST

- It is important to experience how people react to your purpose and vision.
- We recommend the following simple "heart and head" test, which asks two questions:
  A. How does your heart react: what do you feel?
  B. How does your head react: what do you think?
- This gives insight into what people like and don't like and why. For example, do your purpose and vision provide enough clarity, inspiration and direction?
- You want to capture people's initial responses when confronted with the vision, so don't share them in advance. You can use two flip charts to capture the feedback. You can structure the feedback to highlight elements that are strong and need to be kept and elements that need to be improved.

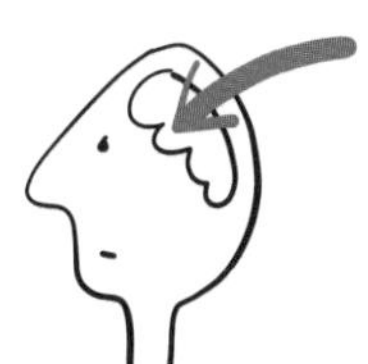

what do you think?
what do you feel?
HEAD
HEART

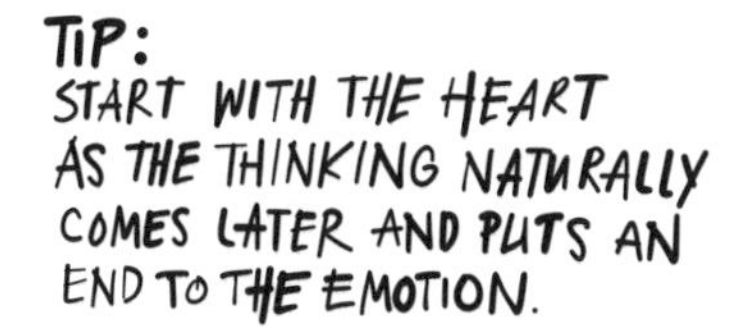
TIP:
START WITH THE HEART AS THE THINKING NATURALLY COMES LATER AND PUTS AN END TO THE EMOTION.

BENEFITS:

- Good way to engage people.
- Visuals trigger constructive responses.
- A vision board allows you to be reminded of it everyday.
- Stimulates people to be creative.
- Provides people with clarity, inspiration, stretch and direction.
- It is the foundation and starting point for goal setting.

4.2 GOAL SETTING
STRATEGIC PLANNING

Envisioning the future is one thing, but if your vision is ambitious enough it will take years of hard work to reach it. As Jack Welch once said, "Good business leaders create a vision, articulate the vision, passionately own the vision, and relentlessly drive it to completion." The question is how to drive the completion of your vision in a rapidly changing world. Faced with this dynamic environment, many companies today are shifting towards more agile organizations. However, Agile does not mean that planning is not important. For instance, in 2016 Mark Zuckerberg revealed Facebook's 10 year roadmap. He used the three horizon approach which plans short term work on core business in horizon 1 followed by options for medium and long term growth in horizons 2 and 3. What Agile means is that you need to be open to adapt these plans quickly based on iterations and experimentation. Visualization is a powerful tool that can help you achieve this.

SETTING THE SCENE

YOU WILL LEARN:

- > **Visual Collaboration Techniques**
- The tree of life
- Road for the future
- User story mapping

WHO typically is involved in goal setting and planning?

- Goal setting and planning happens at all levels of the organization.
- Typically management sets out the corporate goals and strategic plan. Functional and department leaders translate the goals and plan into smaller pieces for the scope of their responsibility. Operational teams make goals and plans for their daily work.
- The finance department facilitates the planning cycle and aligns it with the necessary budget/resources.

WHEN and where does goal setting and planning occur?

- At the highest level, companies set 3, 5 or 10 year planning horizons and have periodic strategic updates, for example every 6 months or every year.
- But at a more operational level you might plan a development sprint for 2 weeks, have daily stand-ups to divide tasks or set daily work schedules in your operations.
- Planning happens throughout the workplace, from the board room to the work floor.

> "I love it when a PLAN comes together"
>
> John 'Hannibal' Smith | THE A team

WHAT happens during the goal setting and planning?

- The starting point is setting goals that motivate and inspire. These goals should meet external expectations and internal capacity to deliver.
- Secondly, you need to understand where you are today – your starting point.
- Thirdly, when planning how to achieve your objectives you try to manage three things: the scope of work, time and resources that are needed to get it done. For instance in an Agile Scrum you mainly focus on the scope of work, as available time and resources are fairly fixed. While on a more strategic level you focus on what resources are needed to get the work done in a certain time frame.

VISUAL COLLABORATION TECHNIQUES

Imagine that you have a vision for the future. Your next challenge is to align people on what needs to be done to get there. This can be at corporate level or for your department or team. Basically, you want to set goals and develop plans. Deciding how to get started and what tools to use depends on the context of your organization and the way you handle change.
There is no one size fits all. Here are some visual techniques that can help inspire your planning processes.

THE TREE OF LIFE

- The tree is an excellent metaphor to visualize your business plan:
  - A. The tree needs water to grow: what resources do you need to invest?
  - B. The tree trunk represents The foundation from which it grows: what are your core values?
  - C. The tree branches illustrate the direction it grows: what are your strategic pillars and goals?
  - D. The apples are the results: what are the benefits you want to achieve?
- The visual helps you summarize and communicate your plan.

Tip: We recommend that you create and own this tree together.

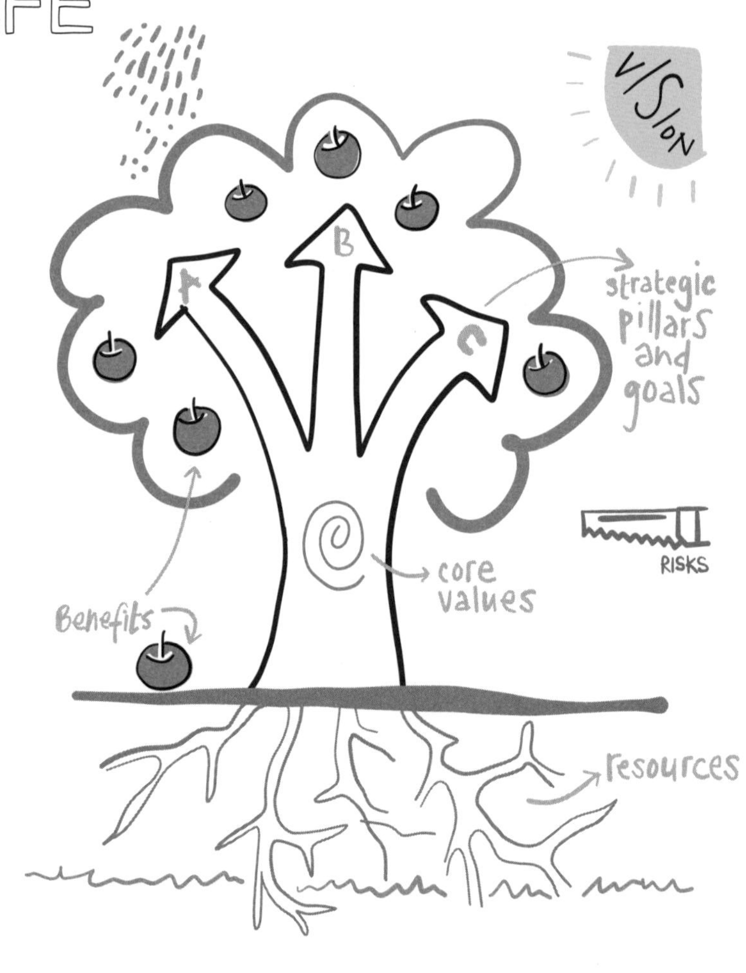

- TIP: make your goals S.M.A.R.T. and use this as a checklist for your plan in separate goal sheets
  - S. Specific: is it clear what I want to do and accomplish?
  - M. Measurable: how do I know that I have achieved it?
  - A. Attainable: do I see myself doing it and can I break it into manageable pieces?
  - R. Realistic: is the goal achievable or too hard/easy?
  - T. Time bound: what is my target date?

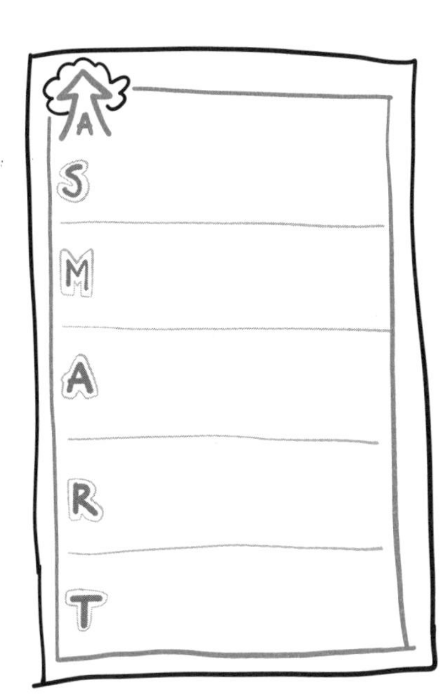

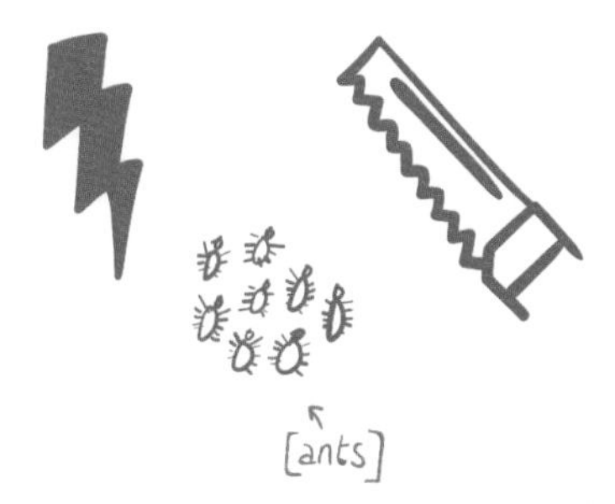

ROAD TO THE FUTURE

- When your vision and goals are clear, a road to the future helps you visualize how you will get there.
- To engage people, you can use a 'brown paper' and sticky notes to develop a plan together.
- Typically you put the vision and goals at the end of the road.
- The steps can be both longer-term strategic horizons or shorter-term tactical and operational steps.
- The steps in the main chart can be underpinned with more details on separate action sheets: For example an action sheet for an initiative that shows the responsible lead, purpose description, targeted value to deliver and team/resources required.

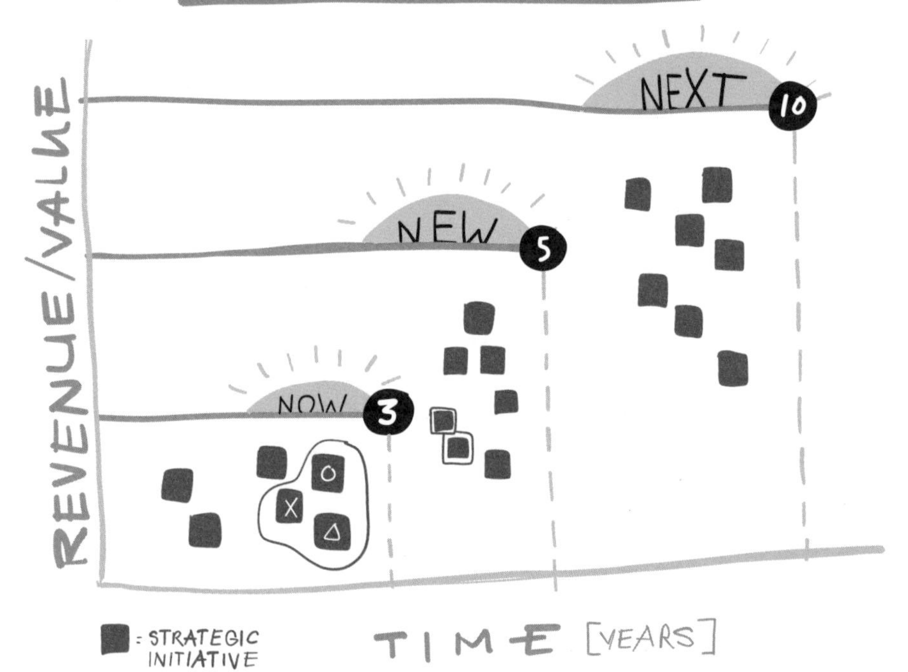

ACTION	WHO	WHAT	WHEN
X	HEAD OF RECRUIT-MENT	ATTRACT 5 NEW UX DESIGNERS	MARCH 2017
O			
Δ			

ALTERNATIVE TEMPLATES

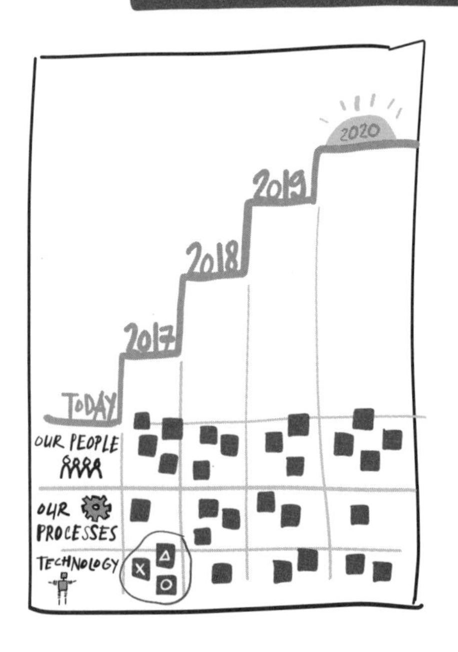

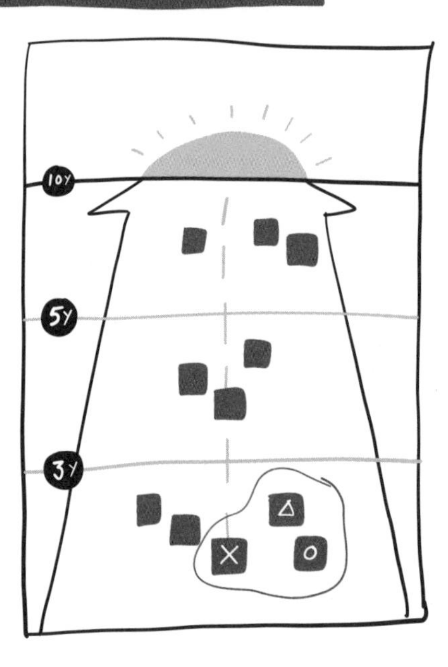

Tip: you can make your road more gripping by adding attributes like potential (road) blocking risks and moments of meaning.

USER STORY MAPPING

- Story mapping is developed by Jeff Patton and helps you create an Agile development map, for example for a new app you want to build. It is an engaging activity where all participants are involved to map the requirements.
- You start by gathering the user tasks: the things people do. For instance in case of an Airline app: “edit user profile”, “book trip” or “request upgrade”. Typically each user task starts with a verb you write on a post-it. This only takes 5-10 minutes.
- Next, the participants will group the tasks which are similar and remove duplicates. Above each group of tasks you can place a post-it of another color and write the name (user activity) on it. Jeff calls this the skeleton of your story map.
- Now you can detail the tasks with user stories related to them. A user story is a simple description of what a user wants: As <perso-na> I want <what> so that I <why>. You can write them on a sticky note with another color for all user stories.
- The last step is the prioritization of the user stories by slicing them from top to bottom into releases/ sprints. Challenge especially the first release to ensure your Minimal Viable Product (MVP) is as thin as possible.
- The story map is not fixed. You can update, reprioritize, add and remove user stories every week.

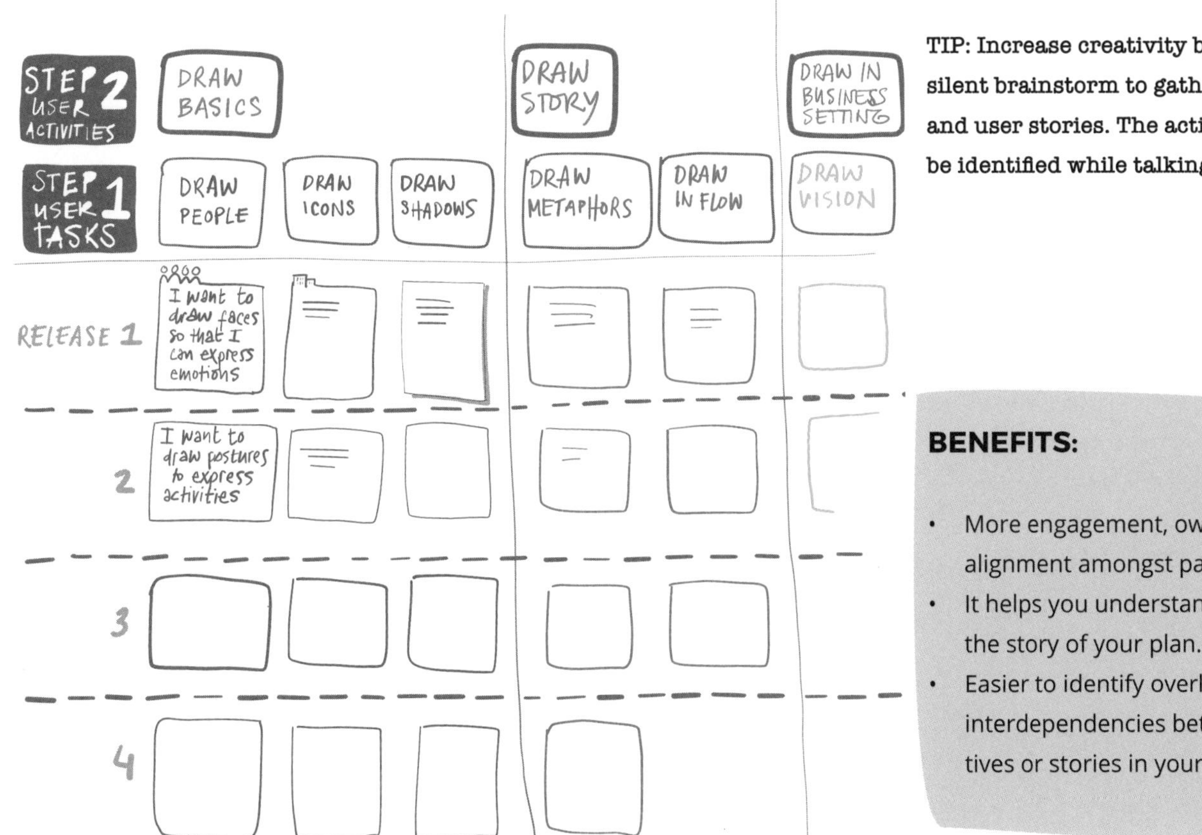

TIP: Increase creativity by using a silent brainstorm to gather the tasks and user stories. The activities can be identified while talking.

BENEFITS:

- More engagement, ownership and alignment amongst participants.
- It helps you understand and tell the story of your plan.
- Easier to identify overlap and interdependencies between initiatives or stories in your planning.

4.3 INFORMATION SHARING
REACH OBJECTIVES

Many businesses organize meetings just to share information. The stand-up is a relatively new form of information sharing and is part of a larger new way of managing projects called the Agile Scrum (developed by Ken Schwaber and Jeff Sutherland) which involves autonomous teams working iteratively and incrementally in short sprints. The stand-up is a business setting where (project) teams gather to synchronize their shared goals and objectives. During the stand-up they give updates on their efforts to reach those objectives and raise concerns over future planned activities.
So, basically, it is a gathering of the whole (project) team for a quick status update. We consider the stand-up also to be an effective tool for sharing information at other layers and settings in the organization. For instance, Spotify uses a "Scrum of Scrums" to share information across teams.

SETTING THE SCENE

WHO typically attends a stand-up?

All (project) team members are required to join the stand-up. In most cases, basically anybody else who wishes to know more about the initiatives of the (project) team and / or contributes to the status and progress of the team objectives is welcome.

YOU WILL LEARN:

- > **Visual Collaboration Techniques**
- Kanban Board
- MosCoW
- T-Shirt Sizing
- Burndown Chart

WHEN and where do stand-up's occur?

Stand-ups follow a "same place, same time" principle. Typically stand-ups are daily and do not take more than 15 minutes. The stand-up takes place where the actual work happens. It is important that all team members stand up during the meeting.

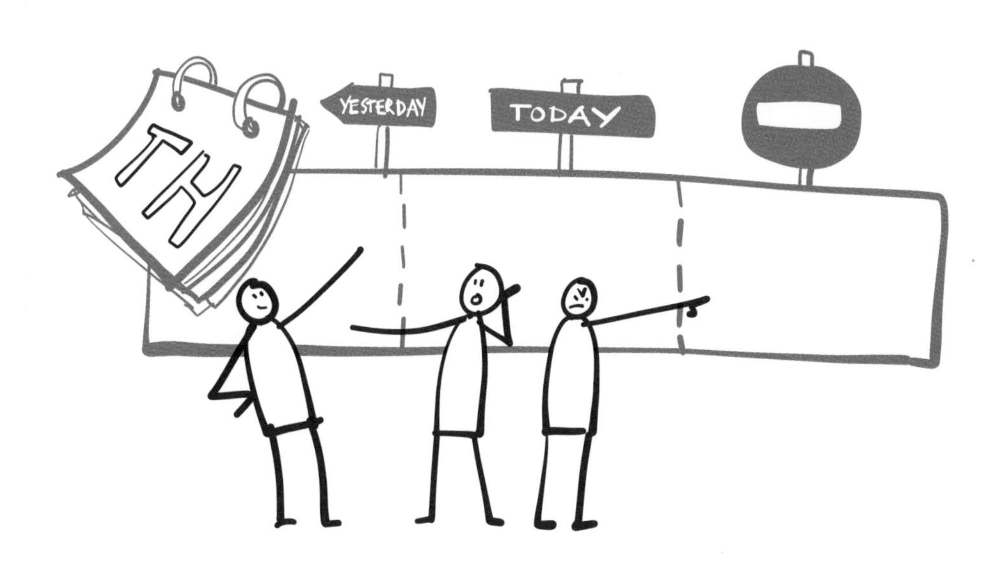

WHAT happens during the daily stand-up?

During the daily stand-up all (project) team members provide an update using a strict protocol that does not allow interruptions. They share what they did yesterday, what they will do today and what is blocking or has blocked their progress. Sometimes people get too talkative and drift into elaborative storytelling, start socializing or try to solve problems immediately after hearing them. That is NOT the purpose of the daily stand-up! If the daily stand-up takes too long energy levels drop and participants will get distracted.

CE-
REC
TOA
CO-CREATE

VISUAL COLLABORATION TECHNIQUES

You are part of a team that gathers in a daily scrum. Imagine, you got into the office just a couple of minutes before the start of the daily stand-up and you are still sipping your coffee. You are wondering how you can change the dynamics of your team's daily routine and make it more meaningful for everybody. Instead of going over the 3 routine questions, you could spice things up by telling your colleagues how you changed the world yesterday, how you will crush it today and how you will blast through obstacles that are standing in your way.

You should also be aware of the following visual thinking and collaboration techniques that could help you and your team

KANBAN BOARD

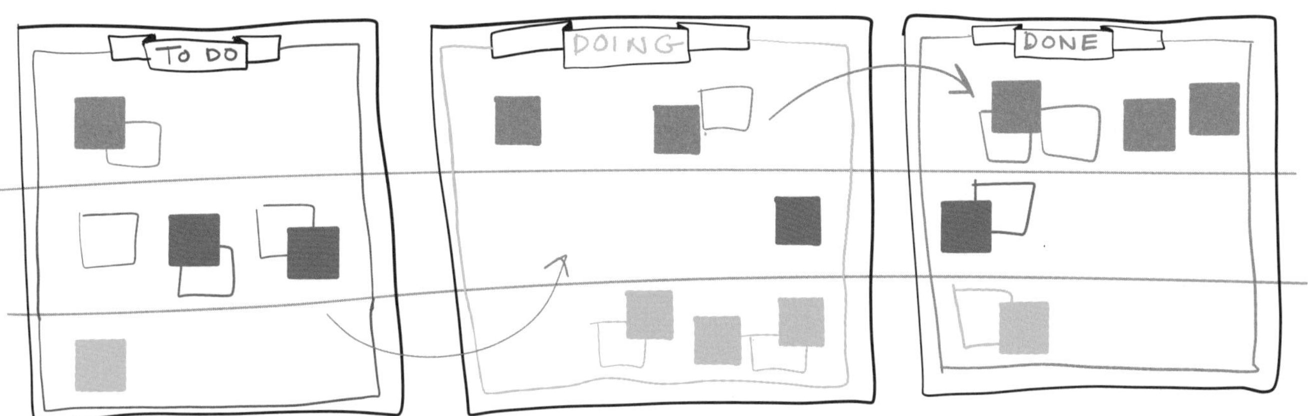

A Kanban board can be used to visualize your team's work and tasks and help your team to optimize the flow of its work. The simplest Kanban Board consists of three columns: to-do, doing and done (inspired by the Toyota Production System). Moving sticky notes from left to right on the board indicates progress. We recommend using various colors of sticky notes to categorize tasks. Be consistent in how you use the sticky notes. Keep the descriptions on the sticky notes short and clear and start with a verb.

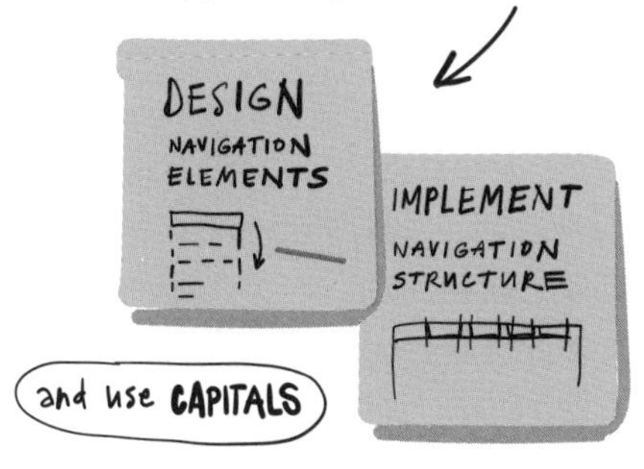

TIP: Avatars don't need to be an exact look-a-like of team members. Teams often use specific themes (eg. movie stars, superheroes, sports-men/women, musical artists. etc.) so that the Avatars illustrate their characters.

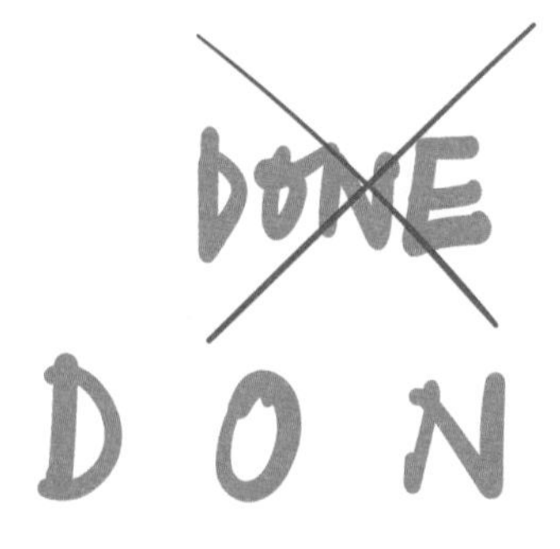

TIP: GIVE EACH LETTER
SPACING IN THE HEADER

MOSCOW: MUST HAVE, SHOULD HAVE, COULD HAVE, WOULD HAVE

The MoSCoW method is a prioritization technique for deciding which user stories to focus on. The acronym stands for: must have, should have, could have, would have. MoSCoW helps you and your team to rank user stories in order of importance to the customer. It creates focus for you and your team and it will increase the chance of delivering a minimal viable product or service at the end of a sprint. It is always a good idea to make sure there are a number of "should-have" and "could-have" items on your Kanban board. It provides your team with some flexibility to finalize work within the agreed upon time frame.

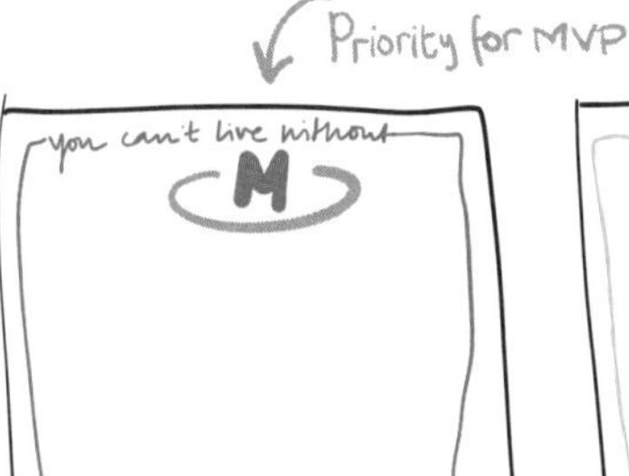

DEVELOPED BY DAI CLEGG

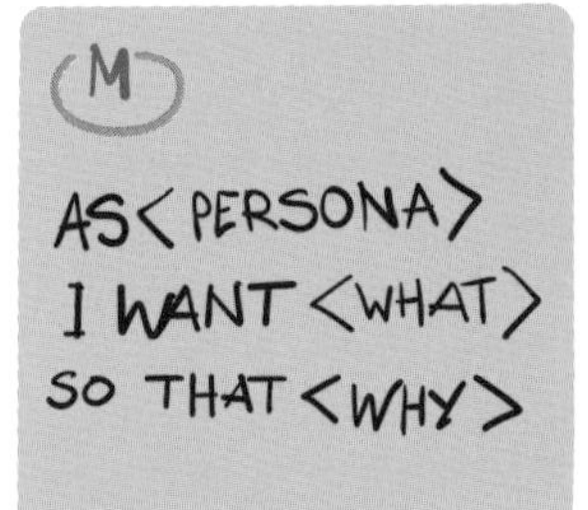

use the same 'logo' as used in big template

SIZE: XS - S - M - L - XL

Use something eye-catching to indicate the effort required to complete user stories or tasks on the Kanban, such as T-Shirt sizes (XS, S, M, L, XL). In order to decide which tasks to prioritize we often just need to understand how big they are in relation to each other, not exactly how many man-hours they will take. By having T-Shirt size cards available for all team members during a daily stand-up you and your team can relatively quickly assess how much effort new tasks require to be completed. This method is based on James Grenning 'Planning Poker' and later popularized by Mike Cohn's book 'Agile Estimating and Planning'.

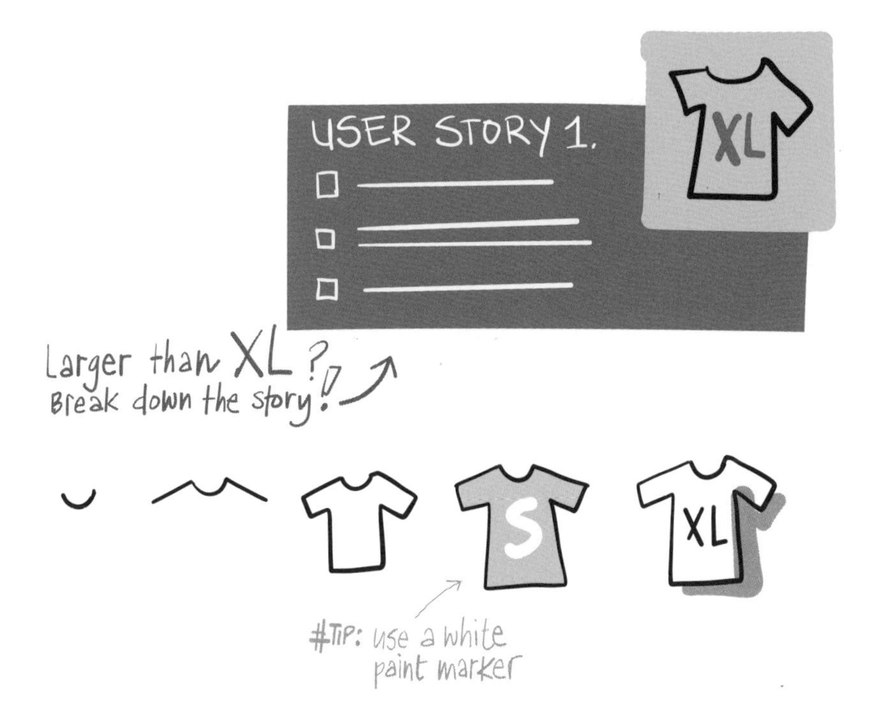

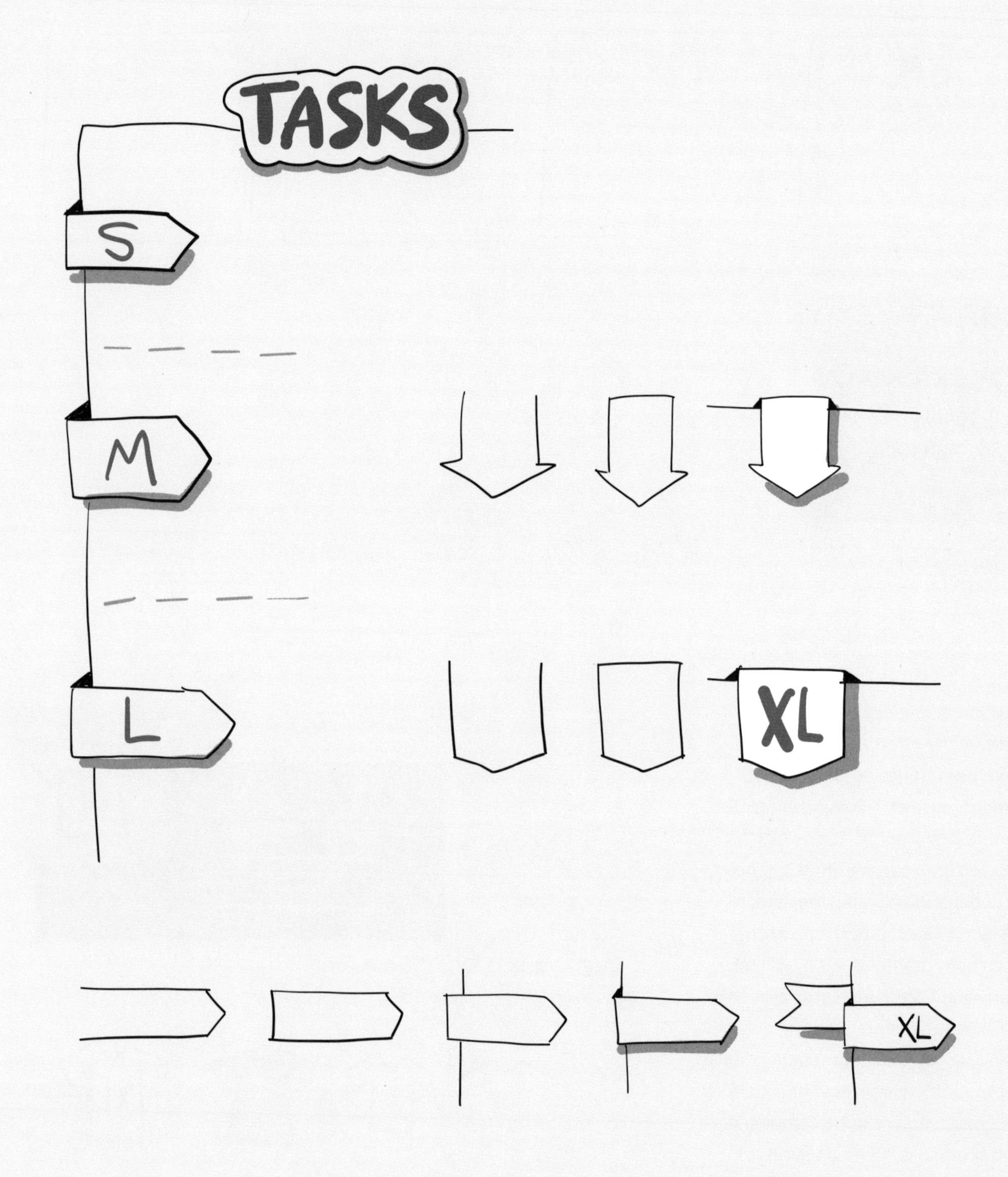

TASKS
S
M
L
XL
XL

BURNDOWN CHARTS

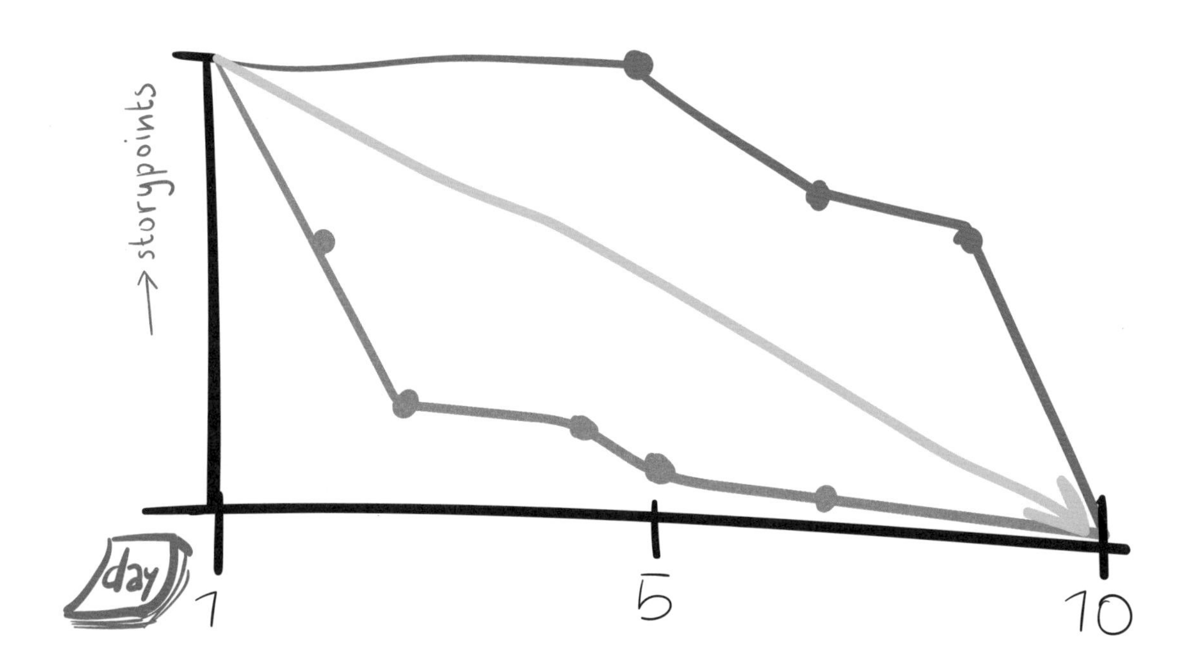

Replace progress reports with a Burndown Chart. Instead of writing progress reports on your computer, create physical burndown charts for your team. The burndown chart is a simple visual tool to track the remaining effort required from a team to complete their workload in a specific time frame. The X axis displays working days (eg. 10 days). The Y axis displays remaining effort (eg. tasks or storypoints). There are 2 lines representing planned progress and real progress. After every daily stand-up, count the number of tasks or storypoints that have moved to "done" on the Kanban Board and update the Burndown Chart.

BENEFITS:

- Physical interaction creates stronger connection to tasks.
- Moving sticky notes is fun and rewarding!
- Personalize work environment (e.g. avatars).
- Meetings are more efficient and less waste is produced.
- Issues raised and tackled faster.

4.4 DECISION MAKING COMPARING OPTIONS

People make decisions every day. Some are life-changing choices, while others are no more than selecting soup from a menu. Robots have even started making some decisions for us. How should we embrace this increased automation, with its opportunities but also threats? This is just one example of the bigger decisions that businesses and policy makers need to make in today's rapidly changing world. And you don't want to make the wrong decision for your business and miss out on a lucrative opportunity. One of the most staggering examples of such a bad decision is Kodak's choice not to commercialize the digital photography technology it invented in the 1980s because the company feared it would destroy it's film sales. Kodak filed for bankruptcy in 2012.

The way you visualize and structure information has a clear effect on the outcome of a decision making process. So using visuals offers a great opportunity to improve your decision-making processes.

SETTING THE SCENE

YOU WILL LEARN:

> **Visual Collaboration Techniques**
Thinking Hats
Option Comparison Table
Decision Trees

WHO typically attends a decision making session?

- Decision making in an organization is ordered around its structure.
- Typically you see that the executive management (CEO, CFO, COO) takes strategic decisions in Management Team meetings.
- Decision making is not only for executives. Team managers and other functional specialists make tactical and operational decisions in their daily work.
- The decision making is often prepared and proposed by employees in the operations and staff departments or by external advisers.

WHEN and where does decision making occur?

- Business decision making mostly happens in formal management team meetings.
- These MT meetings take place periodically, for instance weekly.
- Decision making is often based on a certain amount of uncertainty that you try to limit by gathering facts.
- Issues are decided upon when needed in ad hoc meetings. These can be physical meetings, video conferences or just phone calls.

"Trust your hunches. They're usually based on facts filed away just below the conscious level."

Dr. Joyce Brothers

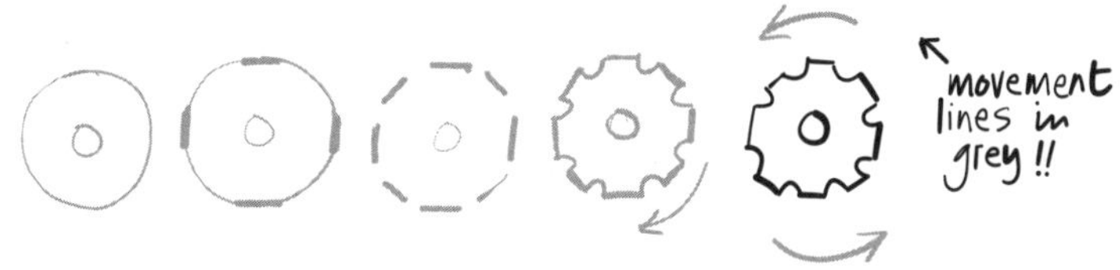

WHAT happens during the decision making process?

- If you don't orchestrate the process, chances are you will end up in spaghetti thinking.
- Typically, business decision making is supported by fact-based techniques to rationalize the decision and mitigate the limitations of human nature.
- A rational decision making involves three steps: 1) determine your objectives, 2) evaluate the options and 3) select the best options.

- The evaluation criteria to reach a strategic decision are mirrored in composition of the management team: a) suitability in the context of the strategy and environment (CEO), b) acceptability from a financial and risk point of view (CFO) and c) feasibility to make it work in practice (COO).

VISUAL COLLABORATION TECHNIQUES

Imagine you are preparing a decision making meeting with the managing board of a company. You have lots of information that has been prepared by all people involved. However, you know the Management Team does not have the time to go through it all. They expect you to guide them through the decision making in an effective one-hour session. How would you go about this? Below you can find our three favorite visual techniques that could help you and your team.

THINKING HATS

- Six Thinking Hats is a concept designed by Edward de Bono.
- Allows you to orchestrate the process by asking everyone to look through the same hat together in a particular sequence. This avoids the natural tendency for muddled “spaghetti thinking” where one person is reacting emotionally (red hat), someone else drops in a creative idea (green hat) while another is thinking objectively about the facts (white hat) and so on.
- You can also divide the hats in a group to get cross-pollination into the debate itself (e.g. optimist versus pessimist).
- You can use physical colored hats to bring a fun element into the group.
- When people get used to the hats their engagement increases. The framework provides a common language and stimulates diversity of thought. It also removes ego and reduces confrontation.

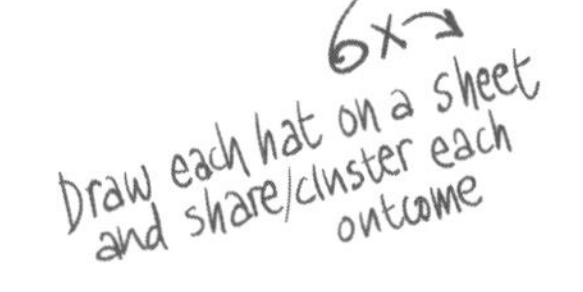

6x
Draw each hat on a sheet and share/cluster each outcome

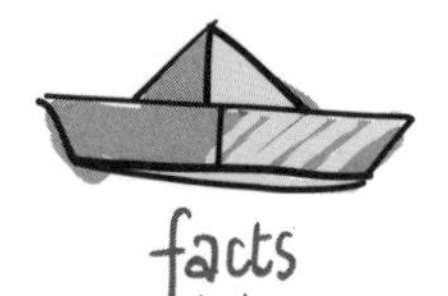

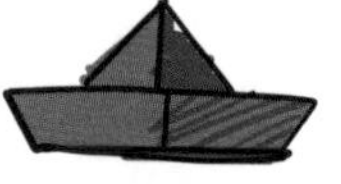

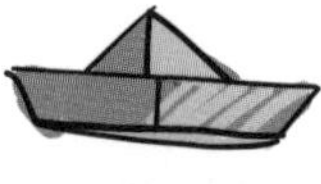

OPTION COMPARISON TABLE

- Allows you to see large amounts of information about the various options simultaneously.
- Allows groupings to emerge as you can easily make comparisons and see relationships between the attributes of the various options.
- Allows you to use symbols, color, size or types of filling to make comparisons more intuitive (e.g. smilies, traffic lights, harvey balls etc.).
- First define the matrix with the options and evaluation criteria, then make the assessment together.
- Less is more... But you need more than one to compare. As a rule of thumb you should aim at 3-5 options and 3-5 evaluation criteria.

TIP: Look for the criteria that display differences between the options and are critial for the decision making.

CRITERIA	A	B	C
BUSINESS SUITABILITY	🙂	😐	🙂
FINANCIAL ACCEPTABILITY	◔	◑	◕
OPERATIONAL FEASIBILITY	●○○○○	●●●○○	●●●●○

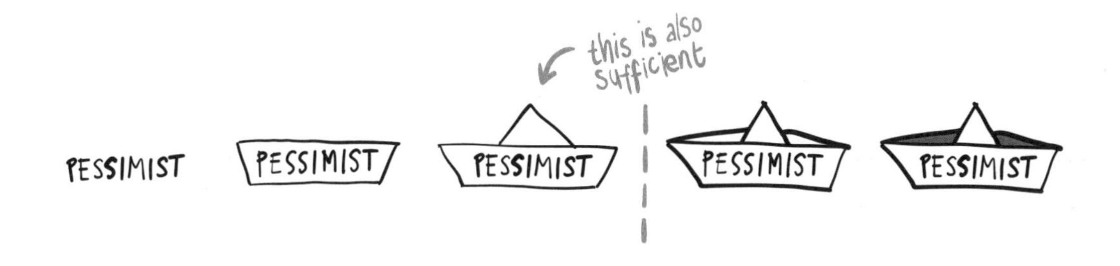

WAYS to COMPARE

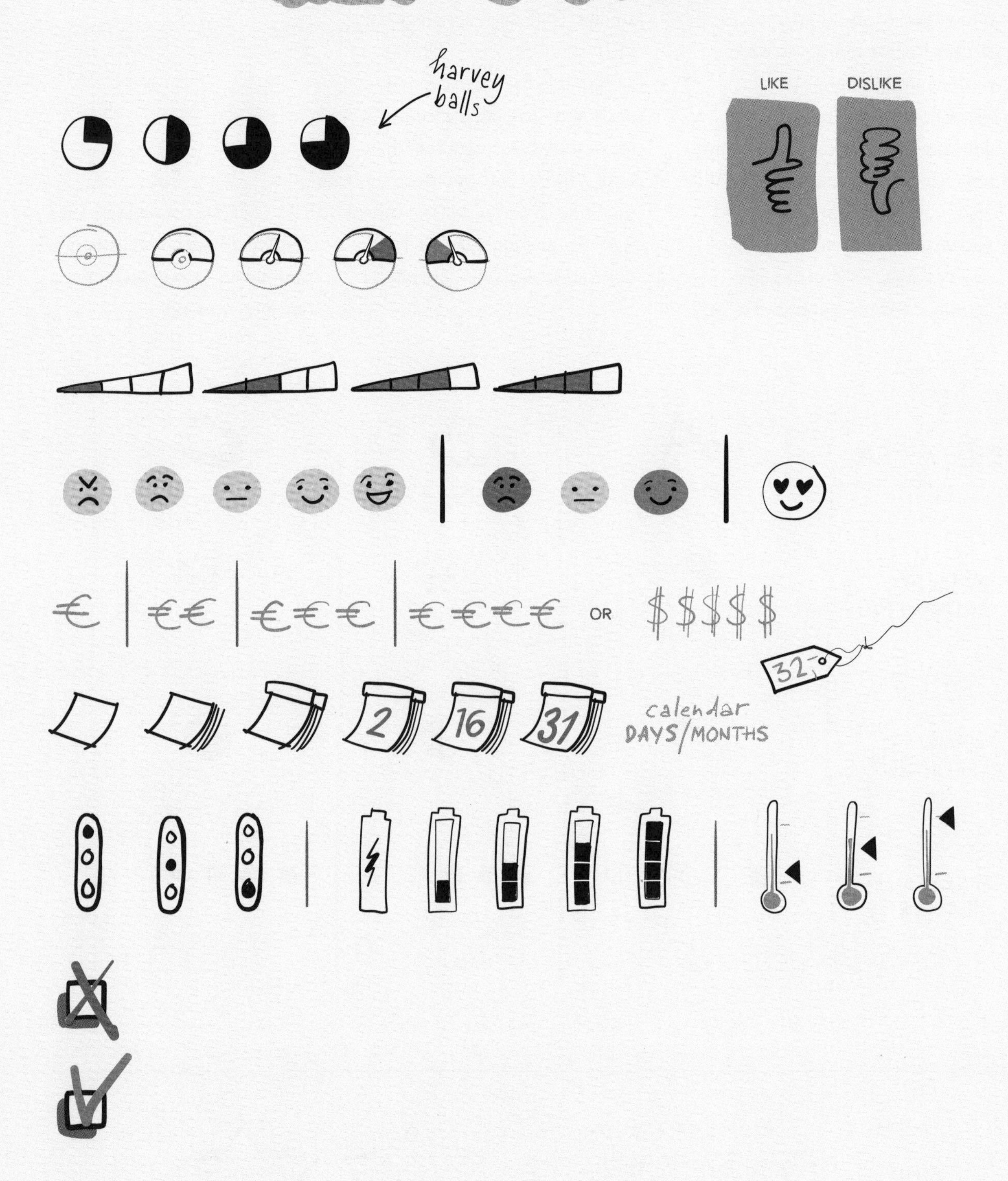

DECISION TREES

- A decision tree is a great way of visualizing potential options and their consequences. It is often used to provide decision makers with guidance or even a protocol.
- First identify the key decision you want to make and phrase it as a question. This is the root node of the tree. Each path from the root node describes a possible future by a sequence of decisions and/or events.
- An example is whether a road maintenance authority should spread salt on roads on a cold winter night. You have two paths: you can decide to preventively salt the roads (cost €10) or wait until snow actually arrives. Last-minute salting is more expensive as you need to call up an additional team (cost €15). The probability of snow is estimated at 40%. In the decision tree you can see that the best decision is to wait as the estimated cost is €6 compared to €10 for preventive salting.

make sure you use different hierarchy in connection blocks [each type of decision]

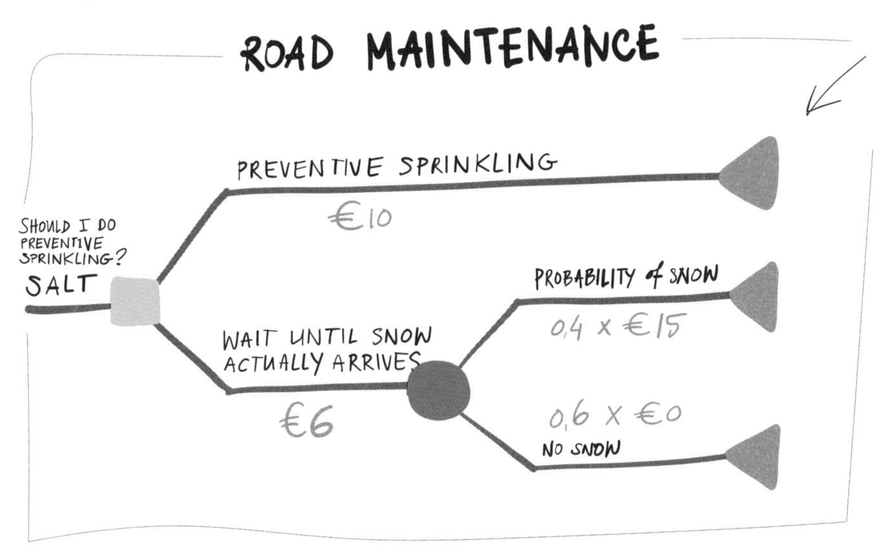

TIP: You can estimate the decision value by combining the probability that an event will happen with the cost/revenue associated with it.

BENEFITS:

- Increase engagement in decision making.
- Remove egos by giving people a "hat".
- Evaluate options across key criteria.
- Provide ability to compare options and see through various alternatives quickly.
- Allow decision makers to understand consequences of decisions.
- Enhance ability to see patterns.

4.5 EXPLORING MARKETS
CUSTOMER INSIGHTS

Nowadays, many businesses are transforming into purpose-led and customer-focused organizations to improve customer loyalty and satisfaction. Essentially, they are trying to convert their customers into fans. A good example is GoPro. GoPro's YouTube channel is full of videos from customers skydiving, skateboarding, skiing and scuba diving. Customers are promoting GoPro's products! To be able to turn customers into fans, it is essential to know your customers and what they want. Visual thinking and collaboration techniques can help you explore markets and create these customer insights.

SETTING THE SCENE

YOU WILL LEARN:

- > **Visual Collaboration Techniques**
- Customer segmentation
- Customer personas
- Customer journey
- Competitive landscape analysis

WHO is involved in exploring markets and creating customer insights?

- For marketeers and data analysts customer satisfaction is an important value or metric for measuring performance. They deal with customers every day and therefore have a good grip on what customers want and how customer needs evolve.
- Marketeers and data analysts also gather insights and data about customer behavior and the competitive environment.

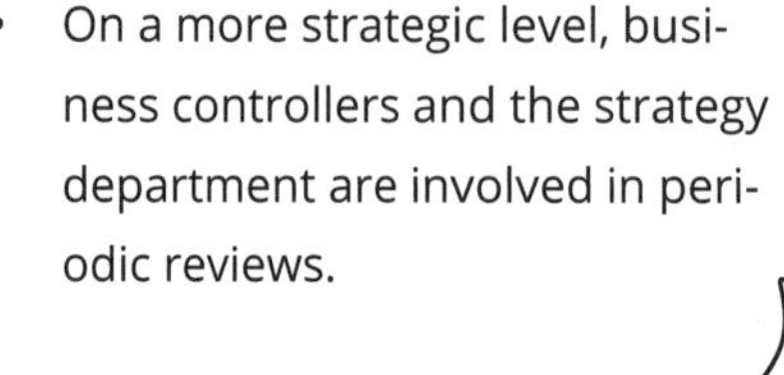

- On a more strategic level, business controllers and the strategy department are involved in periodic reviews.

WHEN and where do you explore markets and build customer insights?

- Many employees who work with customers observe their behavior and needs on a daily basis.
- Customer needs are also captured through digital touchpoints.
- On a more strategic level, periodic reviews (let's say every business quarter) of customer value propositions take place.
- These reviews typically happen in a meeting with managers from various functional areas or even involving customer panels.

CUSTOMER TOUCHPOINTS

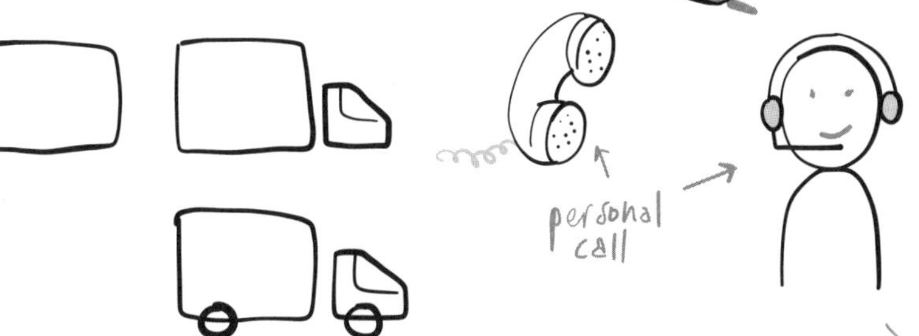

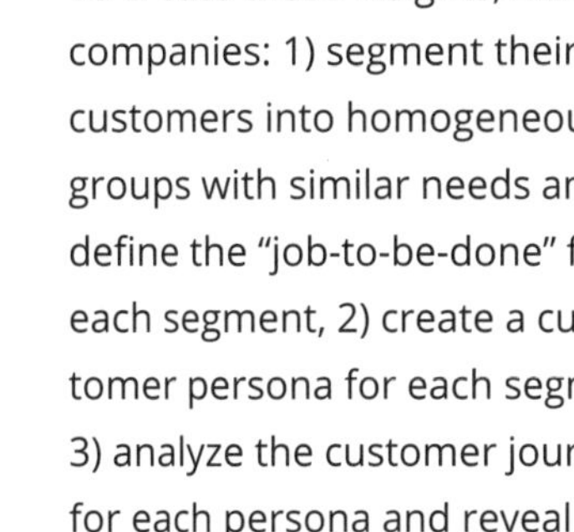

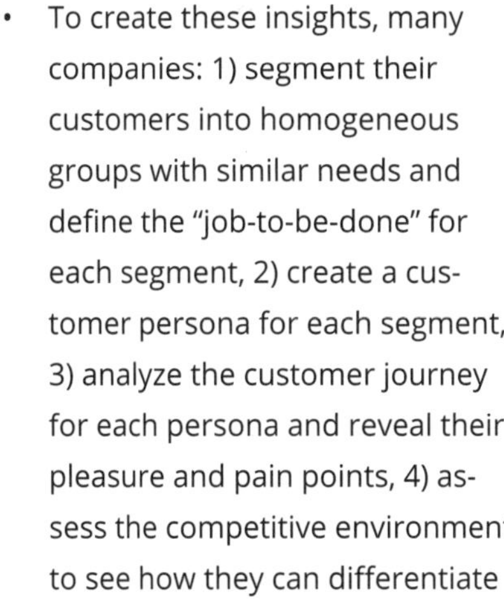

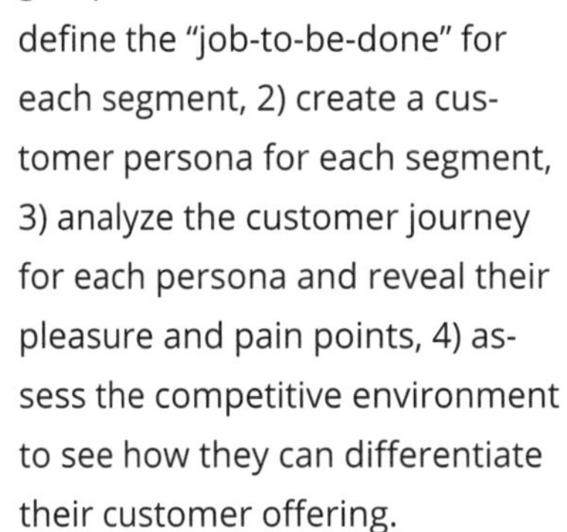

WHAT happens when you are exploring markets and creating customer insights?

- During a strategic review of the customer value proposition you want to create deeper insight into what customers like and where their needs are not being met.
- To create these insights, many companies: 1) segment their customers into homogeneous groups with similar needs and define the "job-to-be-done" for each segment, 2) create a customer persona for each segment, 3) analyze the customer journey for each persona and reveal their pleasure and pain points, 4) assess the competitive environment to see how they can differentiate their customer offering.

VISUAL COLLABORATION TECHNIQUES

Place yourself in the situation that you are part of the team that is responsible for the strategic review of the customer value proposition. Historically, the review has been a painful process within your organization which resulted either in "pie in the sky" ideas or the development of "non-value added gimmicks" for your customers. The reality is that the products that your company offers are not fulfilling the customer needs. You are wondering what you can do differently with your colleagues to create customer insights that can help you to take action and turn customers into fans.

The following visual thinking and collaboration techniques could enable you and your team to create a magic fit between your products and service offer and what customers really want.

CUSTOMER SEGMENTATION AND THE JOB-TO-BE-DONE

- Customer segmentation is helpful in discovering homogenous groups of customers with similar needs.
- Businesses can segment their customers on a variety of factors.
- The most common factors are primary demographic drivers (such as age, gender, etc.), commercial drivers (such as profitability, future value), attitudinal needs (such as self-directed, remote support, face-to-face advice) and product needs (such as basic or advanced).
- It is recommended to start with drawing up 2 by 2 matrices on factors that are important in your business model and customer value proposition and then start drilling down.
- For each segment you can define one or more Job-To-Be-Done's (JTBD), which is a framework that is developed by Clayton Christensen.

TIP: The structure of a good JTBD statement is [action verb] + [object of action] + [contextual clarifier].

Example: Fastfood Restaurant JTBD for a Milkshake: Provide me with [action] easy breakfast/refreshment [object] during boring commute [contextual clarifier].

SEGMENTATION of NEEDS

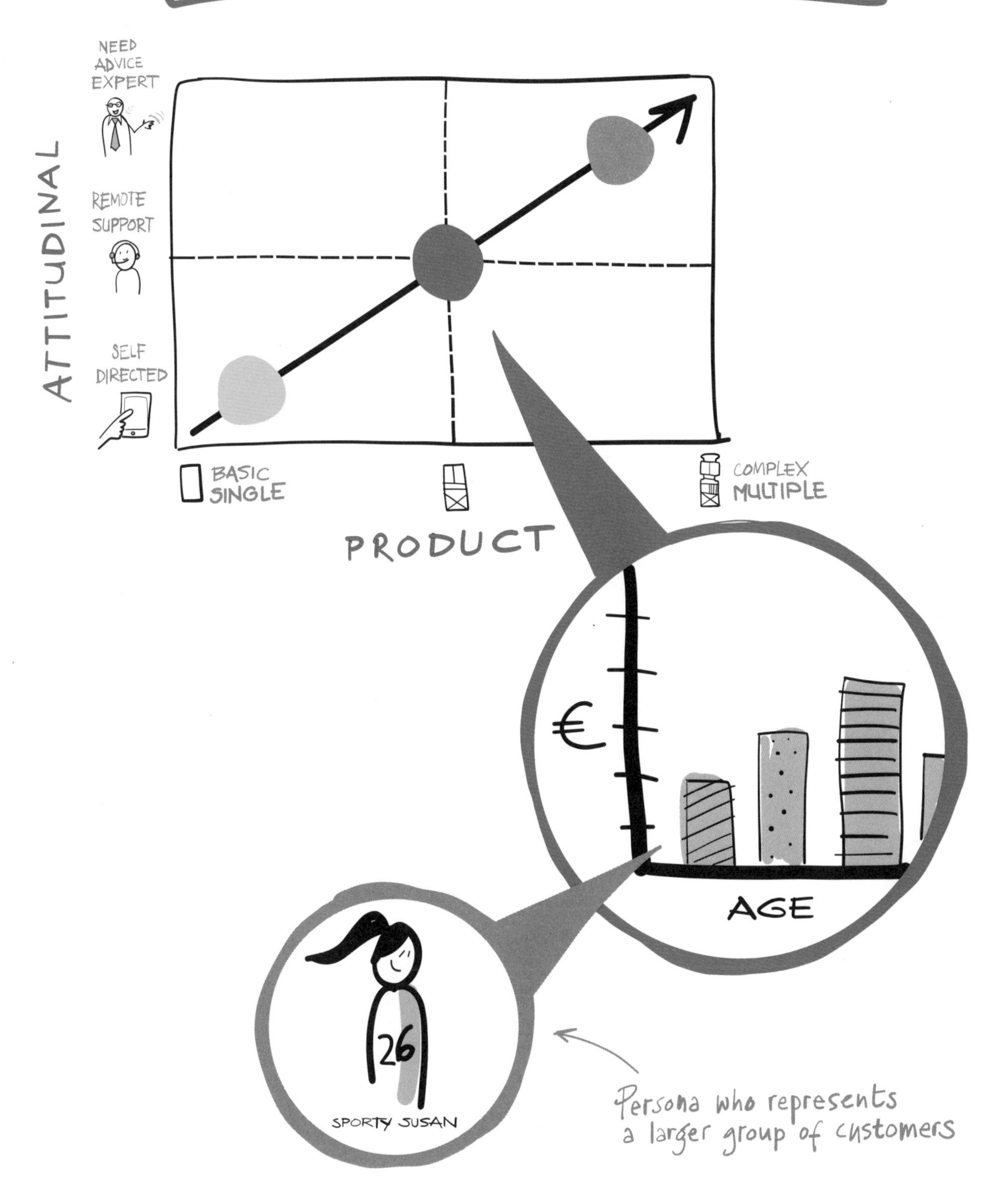

CUSTOMER PERSONAS

The customer persona is a visual of a fictional person who represents a larger group of customers or a segment. The persona helps businesses to better empathize with their customers and find out what they really need. It's important to provide context to the job-to-be-done that helps you in making the problem-solution fit. The persona often consists of; a portrait or avatar, nickname, demographic facts, life quote, a "day-in-the-life" of, description of what is important to them and mood images.

HARDWORKING HENDRICK

MARRIED MONICA

MIDDLE AGED MIKE

HIGH POTENTIAL PENELOPE

SCIENTIFIC STEVE

SPORTY SUSAN

SINGLE STELLA

TODDLER TESSA

CHILD CHELSEA

POLITICAL PETE

HIPSTER HENRY

GRANNY GABRIELLA

TEENAGER TOM

RETIRED ROBIN

MASCULINE MARCUS

CREATIVE CARLA

GRADUATE GWEN

FAMILY MAN FRANKY

CUSTOMER JOURNEY MAPPING AND ANALYSIS

The customer journey map (based on E.K. Strong's AIDA model and popularized in the 21st century) tells the story of a customer experience. It is a visual of what customers do, say, feel and think. It is not the same as a business process. The customer journey often starts long before a company interacts with the customer and it ends with the customer using the product or service after acquiring it. The customer journey map is built in a number of steps. Every customer journey starts with a persona and list the key stages of the experience. Then you list all your customer's steps and interactions with your business. Then you draw the emotional journey and capture love and pain points. Finally you describe what your customer says or thinks during the journey that reveals opportunities to improve the customer experience.

#Tip:
Draw all borders with gray.

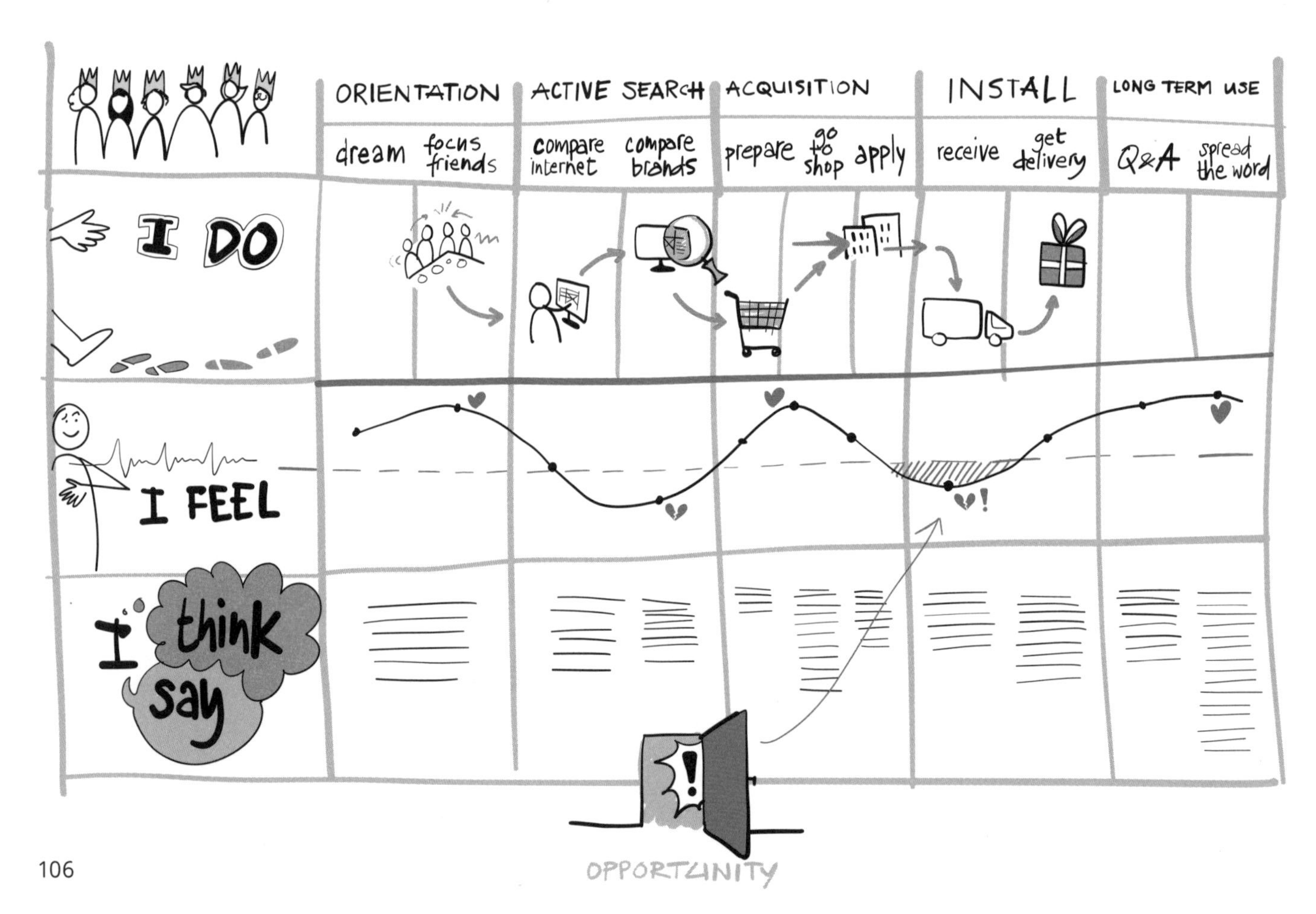

COMPETITIVE LANDSCAPE ANALYSIS

Drawing up the competitive landscape helps you to see how your customer value proposition stands out compared to your competitors. The most common form is to draw a matrix with the brands from your competitors on one end and the key success factors or differentiators with regard to the customer value proposition on the other end. You can bring this competitive landscape to life by using creative scoring mechanisms on key success factors such as price, product features, customer service and geographical reach.

	BRAND A	BRAND B	BRAND C
PRICE	$$	33,-	67,-
FEATURE I II III	●○○○○ ●●●○○ ●●●●○		ok great +/-
	24/7	CLOSED on WEEKENDS	9 to 5
	5,3	4.6 miles average distance to store	

BENEFITS:

- Create a customer-centric attitude and way of working in your business.
- Create deeper and compelling insights into your commercial performance.
- Distinguish different segments and their specific needs from large sets of data.
- Identify opportunities to improve your customer value proposition and experience.
- Create fans of your business!

4.6 IDEA GENERATING DESIGN WORKSHOPS

Idea generating and design workshops are important to innovate your business. Every good idea starts with a challenge. In business the most important challenge is how to meet changing customers needs and drive business success in a world that is constantly changing. You can innovate the experience for your current customers or target a new customer segment that is not served today. To establish this innovation you need to expand your current range of thinking with new ideas. But how do you generate and design these new ideas? And how can visualization help you achieve that?

YOU WILL LEARN:

> **Visual Collaboration Techniques**
Card Mapping
Paper Prototyping
Fiercest competitor

SETTING THE SCENE

WHO typically attends an idea generating design workshop?

- Multiple competences are involved to combine empathy, creativity and rationality.
- Typically, you would involve: marketing, sales, customer support, strategy, product management, UX/UI designers and (R&D) engineers who understand the emerging technological opportunities.

Put the voice of the customer at the center of the IDEA and DESIGN

what does design thinking feel like?

uncertainty / patterns / insight — Clarity / Focus

RESEARCH — CONCEPT — DESIGN

WHAT happens during the design workshop/sprint?

In a design workshop people can feel insecure at first, but with each new idea, the clarity and focus will grow.

The process of designing has subsequent steps of diverging and converging:

A. Getting the right idea: research, generate and prioritize new ideas
B. Getting the idea right: create various concepts for the idea and converge to the right design.

The output is a design which can vary from a very low fidelity sketch to a more sophisticated prototype ready for testing with customers.

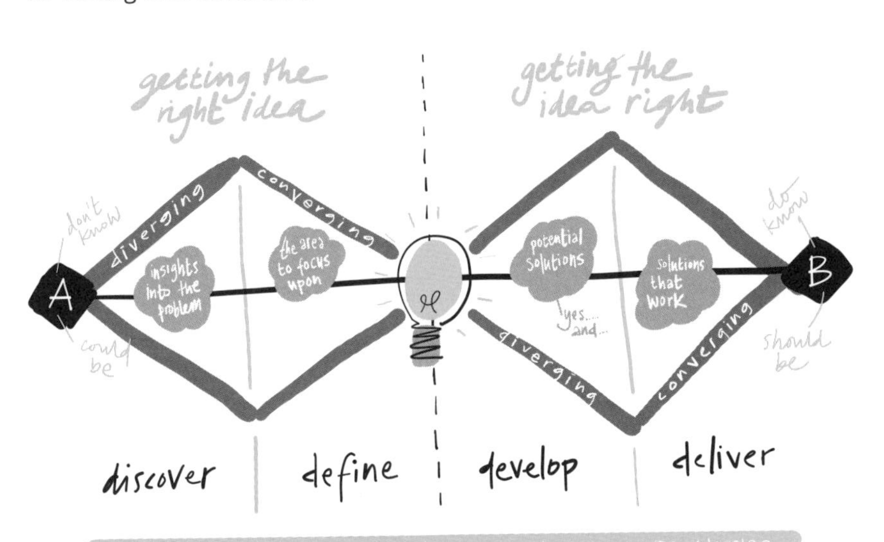

Source: revamped version of the double diamond process by Dan Nessler

WHERE do idea generation and design workshops occur?

- To be held in an environment that triggers creativity and out of the box thinking. Typically these workshops do not take place where people do their routine work.
- The location needs to stimulate creativity and have facilities to engage in design activities (whiteboards, paper, tape, ropes, lego, clay, etc).

WHEN do idea generation and design workshops occur?

Idea generation and design workshops are usually part of the company's innovation challenges or new strategic initiatives. They can last from a few hours to a full week like Google Ventures' SPRINT.

VISUAL COLLABORATION TECHNIQUES

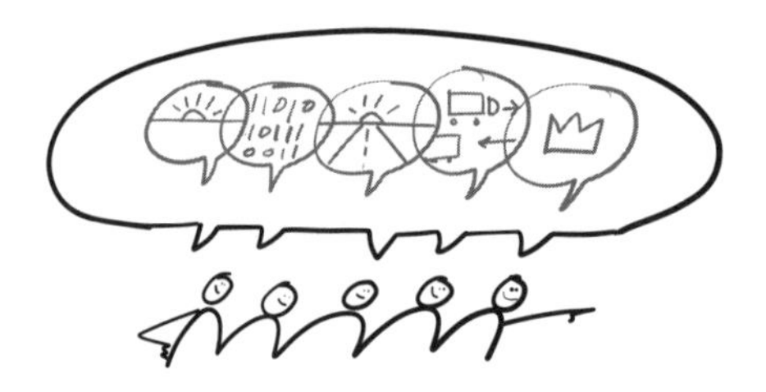

You are part of a team that gathers an idea generation and design workshop. You have been in these sessions before and you noticed that people have difficulties in explaining and building on each other's ideas. This leads to long "no" and "yes...but" conversations and bounds the imagination. You are wondering what you could do to make people share ideas in an effective and inspiring way along a couple of questions: What if? What WOWs? What works? There are some visual techniques that could help you and your team:

CARD MAPPING

- Use time pressure to force people to think without judgement (e.g. 8 idea cards in 5 min.).
- You can use sticky notes to put on a wall or cards to lay down on a table.
- Cluster by grouping ideas and prioritize by visual voting (e.g. dot voting where each person gets 3 labels to stick on their favorite ideas).
- In follow-up iterations, the prioritized ideas will be detailed out and funneled further step by step. Here you can use visual card templates like the Value Proposition Canvas and Business Model Canvas from Alexander Osterwalder.
- Arrange short moments to inject inspiration (e.g. inspirational speaker, case from a company in a different sector or by sharing each other's ideas).

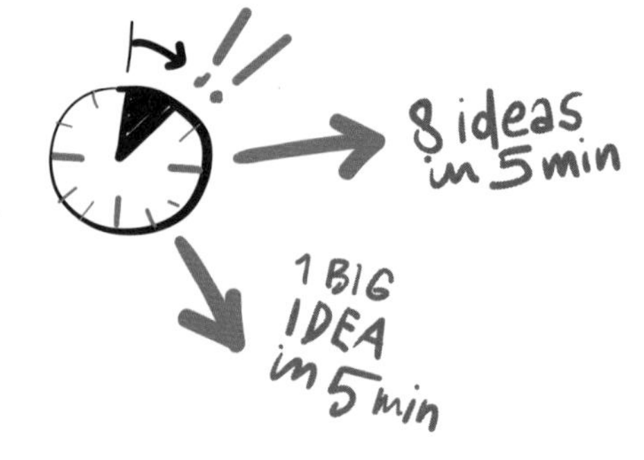
8 ideas in 5 min
1 BIG IDEA in 5 min

1. DRAW A VASE
2. DRAW A WAY TO ENJOY FLOWERS IN YOUR HOUSE
3. SHARE EACH OTHERS IDEAS AND ITERATE TO 3 NEW IDEAS

PAPER PROTOTYPING

Design a paper prototype for a new customer service

- Even a sketch can say more than a 1000 words!
- Especially for designing and testing user interfaces.
- The 'maker movement' opens up entrepreneurship and an urge to experiment.
- Saves time and money.
- Providing paper, pens, tape and other creative materials.
- A wireframe is a design of a website interface. When you are in the ideation phase the wireframe can be sketchy and the fidelity grows via multiple design iterations and testing.

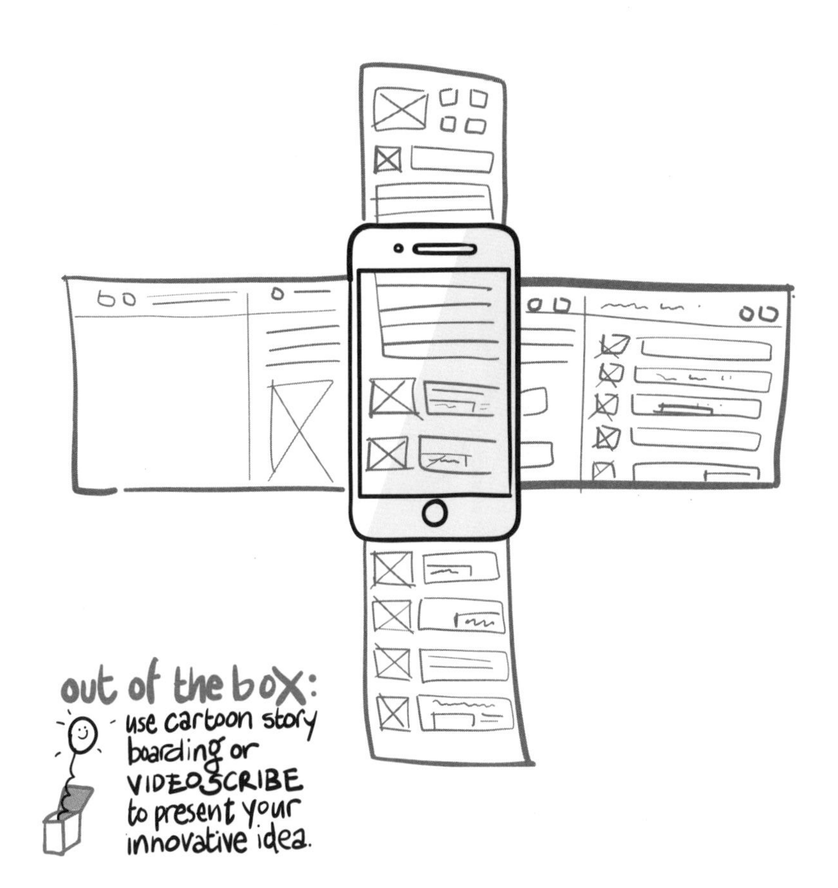

out of the box:
use cartoon story boarding or VIDEOSCRIBE to present your innovative idea.

FIERCEST COMPETITOR

Design your fiercest competitor

- You develop various fiercest competitor scenarios (e.g. a competitor that is leading by technological innovation, sustainability, intimacy or a competitor that is the best place to work for its employees).
- Each team will generate and design a business model for the competitor scenario they are asked to work. Be creative in defining your competitor and his name and logo.
- You can use flip-overs, colours, drawings, metaphors' etc.
- Zen voting: reviewing the ideas and voting in silence. This allows everyone to form their own opinions before they get biased by others opinions.

Make a BIG logo/visual metaphor to strengenth the idea. Let people vote/comment on the ideas.
HERO

BENEFITS:

- Visualisation helps identify relationships between various causes of a problem.
- Visualization extends the memory of the human brain when problem solving and puts everyone on the same page.
- Saves time and money and users feel more comfortable to be critical about something that has not been polished yet.

TIP:
Try silent voting: give feedback without explaining (by sticking red/green dots).

Afterwards let the group explain, and iterate your shared ideas.

#BENEFIT:
get behind the words → the hidden links.

PROBLEM
SOLVING

4.7 PROBLEM SOLVING
CONTINUOUS IMPROVEMENT

Today's world is changing rapidly. From technological breakthroughs like Artificial Intelligence to economic, political and regulatory developments, your business environment never stands still.

While radio took 38 years to build an audience of 50 million. In 2016, Pokomon Go reached 7 million users in 1 week! In this rapidly evolving world, problem solving skills are more important than ever if organizations and people are to adapt and survive.

SETTING THE SCENE

WHO typically is involved in problem solving?

- Everyone is involved in problem solving in their daily lives, including you! However, chances are you are not even aware of it most of the time because it is such an integral part of everyday life and work.
- Problem solving happens at all layers in an organization, from decision-making deep down in the operations to the management board. Typically well-structured problems that happen frequently are handled by lower levels in the organization, while ill-structured, unique problems are tackled by management forming a temporary task force or project team.
- Good problem-solving teams involve all competencies relevant to the challenge.

WHEN and where does problem solving occur?

- Problem solving is not just a skill, it's a mindset in which you continuously challenge the status quo to pro-actively shape your world. So problem solving is not just about dealing with unexpected challenges, it's also about seeing what can

YOU WILL LEARN:

> **Visual Collaboration Techniques**
War room
Fishbone
Tracking board

be improved in the current way of running a business. The latter is often referred to as continuous improvement.

- In practice, problem solving and continuous improvement are most common in teams responsible for resolving incidents in existing operational processes and improving efficiency. These operational teams often work according to a continuous improvement methodology like Lean Management to maximize customer value while minimizing waste. However, continuous improvement can also be applied to commercial teams and other supporting functions in the organization.

WHAT happens when you are solving a problem?

- Problem solving generally starts with the identification of a problem. This is reflected in a problem statement such as: how can we reduce the number of company injuries by 50% in 2017? It is also important to define the related stakeholders, success criteria and solution boundaries/scope.
- Second step is to investigate the drivers (root causes) of the problem.
- The third step is to generate a range of possible solutions (hypotheses) and make a decision.
- The final step is to test and implement the solution, monitor and continuously improve.

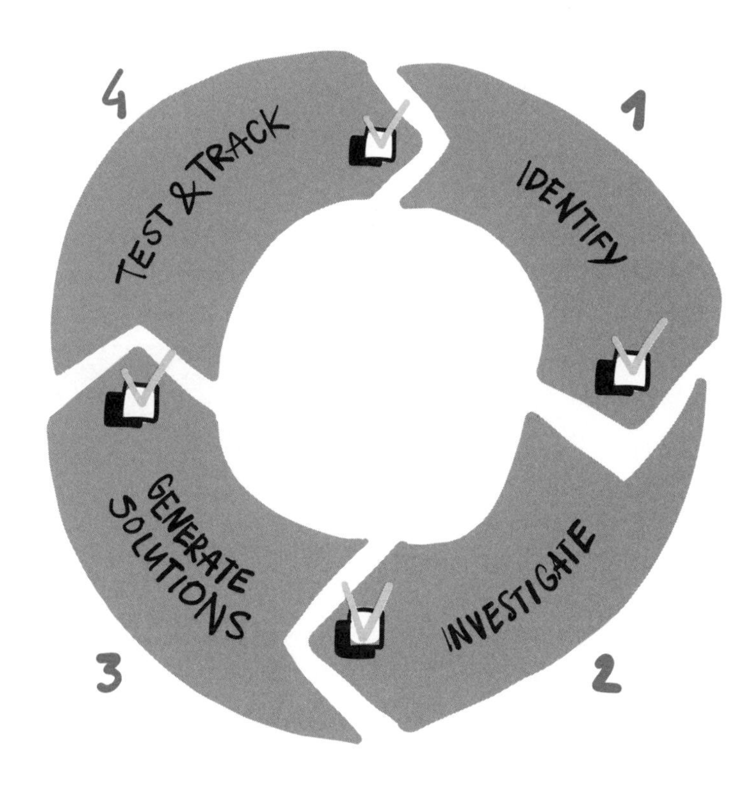

VISUAL COLLABORATION TECHNIQUES

Imagine you have been appointed within the company to address the problem of decreasing customer satisfaction. It's clear that you cannot solve this problem alone and you need to involve others across all departments in the organization.

How can you mobilize and run an effective task force that is going to solve the problem quickly?
There are some visual techniques that could help.

WAR ROOM/ COLLABORATION ZONE

When problem-solving you need to track a lot of moving parts. Having a dedicated war room is a simple trick to bring focus and facilitate the team work. As your human memory is fairly limited, the whiteboard walls can extend the teams memory. By sharing and structuring information on the walls you are creating a shared understanding of what's going on.

Whiteboards top to bottom! On the walls you capture decisions and it's easy to make changes (e.g. reorganize a cause & effect diagram with post-its).

a collaboration zone for large scale problem solving

When too many people are involved to fit into one room, you can create a "collaboration zone". Basically it's a war room at scale. In a collaboration zone you put everyone involved in the task force physically in one place, for instance an entire floor of an office building. You make visually clear who works where (e.g. with team names hanging on the ceiling) and information is captured and shared by all teams on whiteboards/ walls throughout the zone.

FISHBONE CAUSE & EFFECT DIAGRAM

originally developed by Kaoru Ishikawa

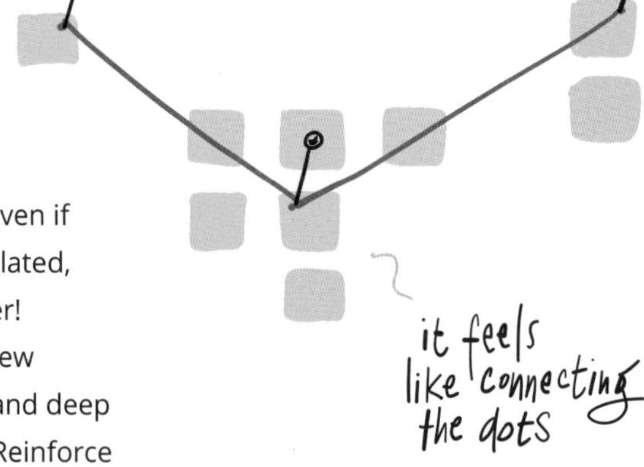

Cause & effect diagrams (e.g. mindmapping, fishbone, logic trees)

- A cause & effect diagram is a tool that helps you understand the issues that could have caused a problem, before you start thinking about a solution.
- You typically use sticky notes to capture the various causes so that you can restructure them easily when necessary.

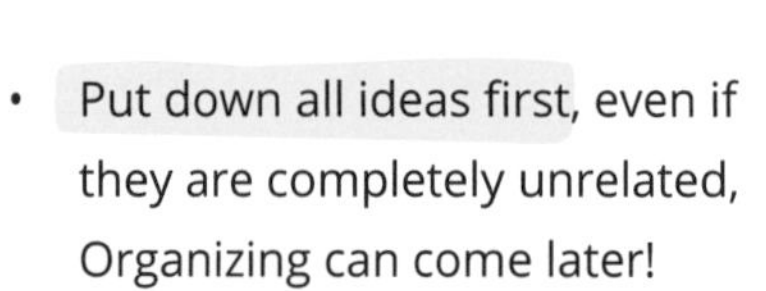

- Put down all ideas first, even if they are completely unrelated, Organizing can come later!
- After that, continue in a few iterations of structuring and deep dives on certain causes. Reinforce the creative process to get all possible causes on the wall.

CONTINUOUS IMPROVEMENT TRACKING BOARD

- Putting a tracking board into the workplace enables real-time engagement. Employees can see how far they are with the improvement.
- Typically you use a whiteboard.
- Often used in Lean (manufacturing) environments.

for example: PRODUCTION SCOREBOARD, kanban, safety board, Continuous improvement Tracking Board.

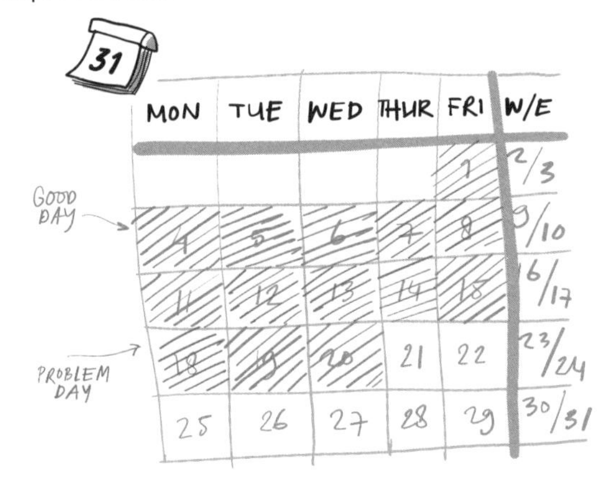

	MON	TUE	WED	THUR	FRI	WKND
JANET						
BILL						
TOM						
SASKIA						

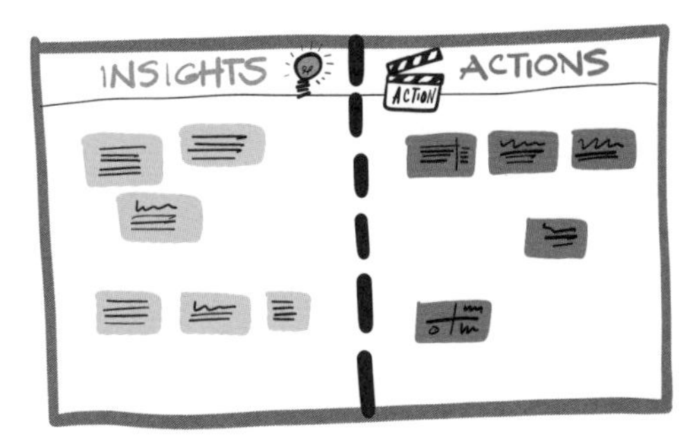

ISSUES & PROBLEMS

9/11	9/12	9/13			
9/12	9/13	9/14	9/18	9/21	
9/8	9/14	9/10	9/12		
9/11	9/14	9/18	9/21		

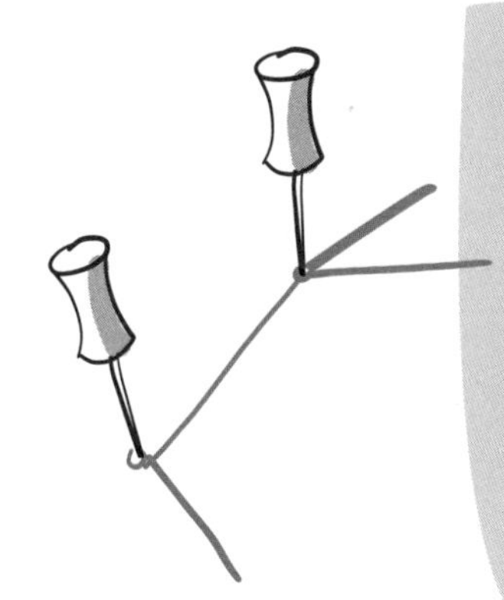

BENEFITS:

- Interactive way of engaging people and letting them contribute to the process.
- Enhances understanding and helps identify relationships between various causes of a problem.
- Visualization extends the memory when problem solving.
- Keeps everybody up to date on progress.
- Makes continuous improvement tangible in the work environment.

4.8 PROTOTYPING EXPERIMENTING

Many businesses have changed their approach to developing new products or services from traditional waterfall to approaches like Lean Startup, Design Thinking and Agile Scrum. Instead of following a step-by-step approach to launch the perfect version of a new product, these new Build-Measure-Learn approaches are all about failing fast. They use rapid prototypes and experiments to maximize learning.

Develop a minimal viable product (MVP), quickly test it in the real world, collect customer feedback, learn and use that knowledge to build something better. Then repeat this cycle to create something that your customers will truly love.

For instance: Zappos (the largest US online shoe retailer) started its business by posting pictures of shoes from local stores online. Each pair of shoes they sold through their website, they had to go and buy from the shoe store and then ship them to the customer. That way, Zappos measured their initial success, learned what customers really wanted and continued to build what today is a billion dollar business.

YOU WILL LEARN:

> **Visual Collaboration Techniques**
Minimal Viable Product
Event Canvas
Product Experiment Board

SETTING THE SCENE

WHO typically is involved in prototyping and experimenting?

Building an MVP and completing the Build-Measure-Learn cycle requires collaboration of multiple disciplines within a business. Most often the team that is looking to develop new products or services includes people from: Marketing, Product Management, R&D, IT, Sales, Marketing and Product Management. Together they form hypotheses around a new product or service offering. R&D and IT develop a prototype. Sales representatives design and execute an experiment to collect customer feedback and measure customer behavior.

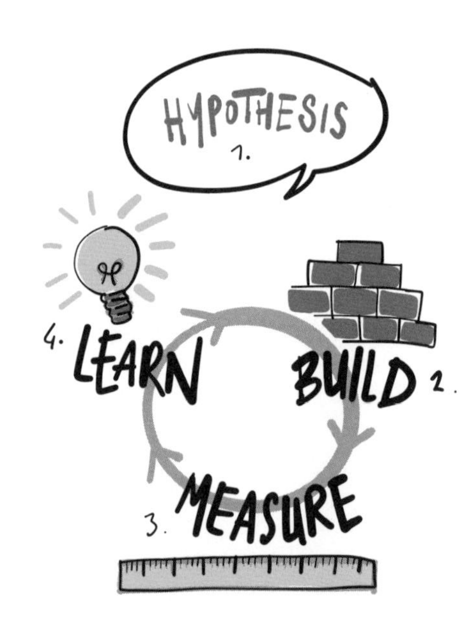

WHEN and where does prototyping and experimenting occur?

The Build-Measure-Learn approach comes from the Lean Start-up method and is a continuous process of refining a product or service offering.

For many teams it resembles their daily way of working. It is important to note that this process is iterative, short-cycled and that a large part of the process happens outside of the office, preferably where your customers are.

WHAT happens when you are prototyping and experimenting?

So the Build-Measure-Learn approach is a cycled process that teams follow to refine, improve or quickly steer away from ideas for new products or services. During the Build-Measure-Learn cycle, you 1) generate a series of hypotheses about an idea for a new product or service 2) build a minimal viable product or design a service prototype 3) set up an experiment in the real world to measure customer reactions and collect feedback 4) capture insights and lessons learned to form new hypotheses.

VISUAL COLLABORATION TECHNIQUES

You are part of a team that is looking to implement a new product or service. In the past you and your team used to begin with an idea thinking you knew exactly what your customers needed.
Then you would spend months (or even years) with your team to plan, design and develop the "perfect" product. However after launching it you discovered that your customers are actually not interested or that a competitor has already launched a similar product. Now, you are looking to introduce the Build-Measure-Learn approach into your team to iteratively develop and experiment with prototypes of a new product or service and lay down a learning path towards achieving a great product-market fit. The following visual thinking and collaboration techniques can help you and your team to adopt the Build-Measure-Learn approach.

PROTOTYPE AND MINIMAL VIABLE PRODUCT

Prototypes and MVPs are common ways of testing hypotheses and ideas for new products and services in the real world. They allow you to learn and get useful insights to develop solutions with a good product-market fit. Basically they boil down to the same thing, but there are some differences. A prototype demonstrates an idea for a new product to see if it is viable. An MVP is a first version of your product that can be launched with just enough functionality to be considered useful for receiving customer feedback. The prototype/MVP board could help you and your team capture your team's ideas and hypotheses for new products or services and decide on an appropriate prototype or MVP. The Prototype or MVP can be anything from paper drawings (low-fidelity) to something that you can physically touch or that allows click-through of content to a fully functioning site (high-fidelity). Make sure to agree with your team on the type of prototype or MVP that you are going to use to test your ideas before investing resources into development.

HOW TO BUILD A MINIMUM VIABLE PRODUCT:

FRAMEWORK developed by Frank Robinson, Steve Blank, Eric Ries a.o.

Source: Henrik Kniberg

The Flintstone:
(aka Wizard of Oz; aka The Mechanical Turk): Design a front-end webpage that looks like a fully functioning online product, while in reality your services are being carried out manually.

The Hotel Concierge:
Find customers who are really interested in the concept of your new product and give them concierge treatment by providing them services manually that represent exactly the same steps that people would go through for your product.

The Fundraiser:
Make a short 1 or 2 minute video that explains the concept of your new product and launch a crowdfunding campaign to develop the product.

The Fake Door:
(aka The Fake Menu): Simulate having a new product or service on the shelf, without actually having it, simply to check if there is any customer interest.

The Pinocchio:
Make a non-functional, life-less version of your product to get feedback on form, shape and usability.

Re-Label:
(aka The Impersonator): Change the label or packaging of an existing product or service to test if customers are interested.

The Stripped Tease:
Create a low-fidelity version of your product with limited functionality to test customer reaction.

"DEVELOP A POLISHED PRODUCT and people only see flaws.....
DRAW A RAW PROTOTYPE and people only see potential....."

PROTOTYPE / MVP BOARD

PRODUCT NAME
DANCE-DANCE.COM

JOB-TO-BE-DONE
ENTERTAINING & EDUCATIONAL DANCING GAME

METRICS
- # downloads
- ranking dancing apps
- daily active players
- session length

TARGET GROUPS
8-12 YRS
- children 8-12 year
- focus on girls ♀
- interested in music & dancing
- play games
- Ipad / Iphone

BIG PICTURE
- IPAD APP
- CHARACTERS
- VIRTUAL DANCE FLOORS
- LEARN MOVES 1→3→2-1
- DANCE WITH OTHER FRIENDS ONLINE (MULTIPLAYER)
- GET POINTS 9 10

PROTOTYPE / MVP
1.0
- FREE APP
- LIMITED IN APP PURCHASE
- BASIC FUNCTIONALITY

2.0
- FACEBOOK INTEGRATION
- MULTIPLAYER

3.0
- PURCHASE MOVES
- CREATE CHOREOGRAPHY

4.0
- NEW FLOORS
- CONTEST / COMPETITION

EVENT CANVAS

The #EventCanvas is a visual collaboration tool that helps your team systematically design effective events.

It's a helpful tool to visualize an event's potential (it's promise to change behaviour) of a variety of stakeholders, how it helps to get their jobs done and against which trade offs.

LEARN BUILD MEASURE

The team process allows everyone involved in the event to get on the same page using visual thinking. In the design process, you first define the "Change" of behaviours from entry to the exit of the event.

Then you "Frame" the event by adding all the restrictions (think cost/revenue, commitment in time and expected return). Lastly the team creates multiple and iterative "Prototypes" of the actual event Experience Journey and Instructional Design.

The first 100 pages of the Event Design Handbook (Frissen, Janssen & Luijer, 2016, BIS Publishers) and the #EventCanvas (under a Creative Commons 4.0 license) are available for download at www.eventcanvas.org.

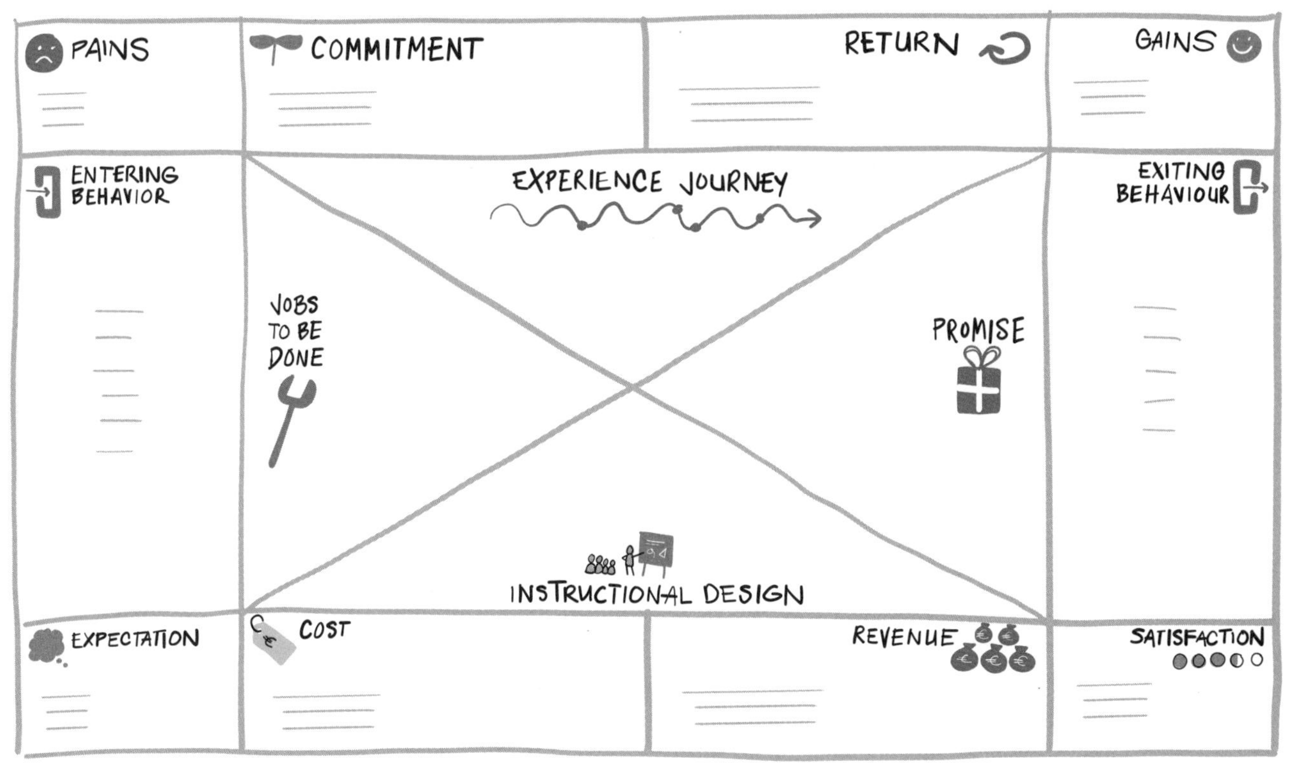

PRODUCT EXPERIMENT BOARD

The product experiment board provides a simple structure for your experiments. It encourages you and your team to follow a structured process to explore creative ideas for new products and services. You record content on the board as you go down each column. This can be easily accessed later as you tell your story. Begin by establishing your riskiest- or "leap of faith" assumptions. Then proceed to generate key hypotheses for these assumptions. For each hypothesis, document potential experiments to run, including measurable behaviors and target metrics. Once your experiment is completed, you can visualize your results as well as new learning and insights. Finally, you can use this new "data" to make your next decision, and the process repeats itself. As you record each experiment, the experiment board records your progress.

Tip: Put all the content on sticky notes, then place the notes in the corresponding boxes. The small size of the sticky notes forces you and your team to phrase answers concisely and encourages you to break down problems and hypotheses into small parts.

back to the
drawing
BOARD

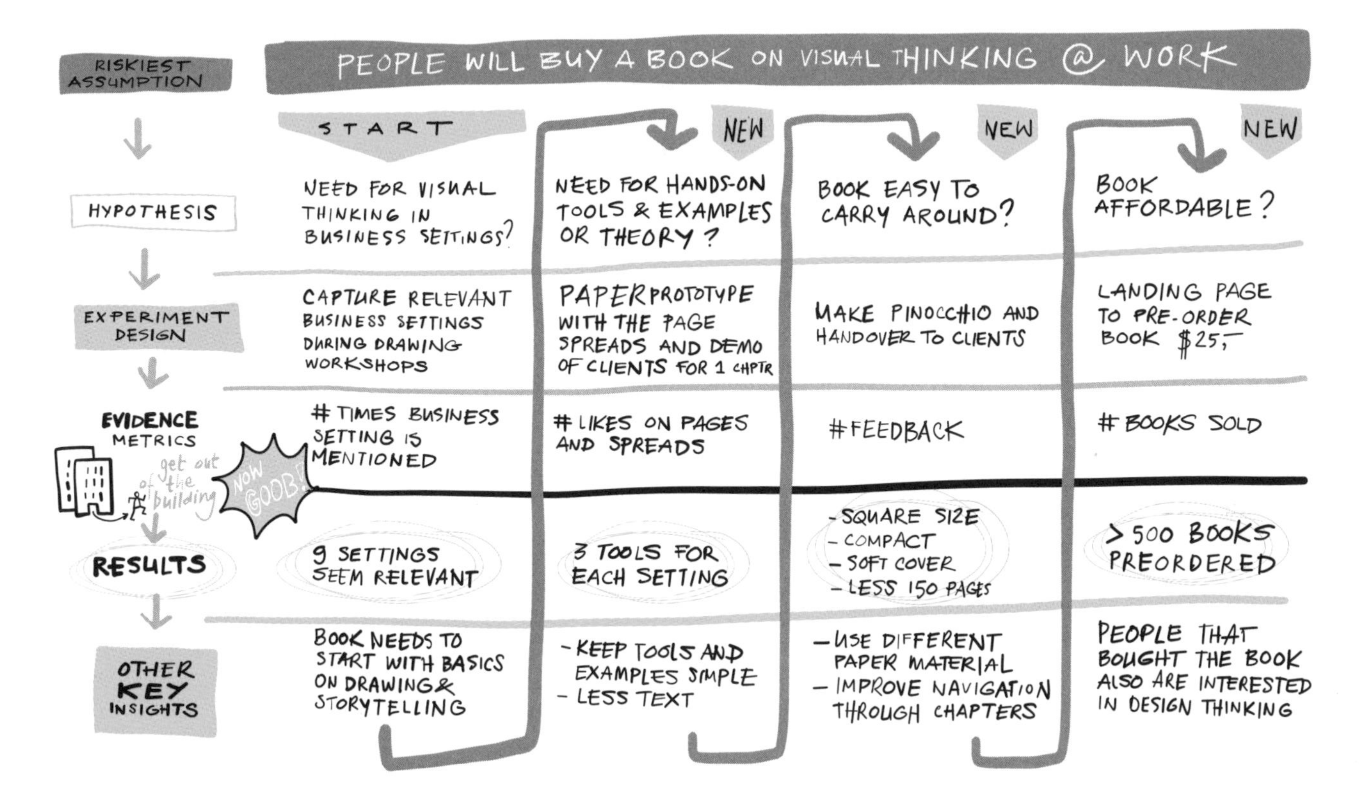

EXPERIMENT BOARD
RISKIEST ASSUMPTION
PEOPLE WILL BUY A BOOK ON VISUAL THINKING @ WORK
START
NEW
NEW
NEW
HYPOTHESIS
NEED FOR VISUAL THINKING IN BUSINESS SETTINGS?
NEED FOR HANDS-ON TOOLS & EXAMPLES OR THEORY?
BOOK EASY TO CARRY AROUND?
BOOK AFFORDABLE?
EXPERIMENT DESIGN
CAPTURE RELEVANT BUSINESS SETTINGS DURING DRAWING WORKSHOPS
PAPER PROTOTYPE WITH THE PAGE SPREADS AND DEMO OF CLIENTS FOR 1 CHPTR
MAKE PINOCCHIO AND HANDOVER TO CLIENTS
LANDING PAGE TO PRE-ORDER BOOK $25,-
EVIDENCE METRICS
TIMES BUSINESS SETTING IS MENTIONED
LIKES ON PAGES AND SPREADS
FEEDBACK
BOOKS SOLD
get out of the building
NOW GOOB!
RESULTS
9 SETTINGS SEEM RELEVANT
3 TOOLS FOR EACH SETTING
- SQUARE SIZE
- COMPACT
- SOFT COVER
- LESS 150 PAGES
> 500 BOOKS PREORDERED
OTHER KEY INSIGHTS
BOOK NEEDS TO START WITH BASICS ON DRAWING & STORYTELLING
- KEEP TOOLS AND EXAMPLES SIMPLE
- LESS TEXT
- USE DIFFERENT PAPER MATERIAL
- IMPROVE NAVIGATION THROUGH CHAPTERS
PEOPLE THAT BOUGHT THE BOOK ALSO ARE INTERESTED IN DESIGN THINKING
BASED ON WWW.LEANSTARTUPMACHINE.COM

BENEFITS:

- Quickly generate evidence for (or against) ideas for new products and services.
- Discover problems inherent to new ideas before investing significant amount of resources.
- Get real answers from real customers early in the process for product development.
- Transform opinions into facts, so you can make better and faster decisions.
- Dramatically reduce the risk and uncertainty associated with new ideas.

4.9 TEAMBUILDING
TEAM PERFORMANCE

A team is a group of individuals that works toward a common goal. A high-performing team builds on that foundation. Its members have a deep trust and respect for each other and are committed to achieving their goals. They clearly define their roles and responsibilities, communicate frequently and share direct and open feedback. A high performing-team often is made up of agile individuals with different ways of thinking and a diversity of skills who feel empowered to take ownership of an issue and can adapt quickly to change.
For instance: Pixar, the movie studio that produced blockbusters like Toy Story, The Incredibles and Monsters Inc. is famous for their high performing team culture. They recognized that in a world that becomes mobile first, the actual face to face conversions threatened to disappear. Pixar emphasized that it is important that teams sit together, get to know each other, invest in relationships and have face-to-face interactions to spark ideas. Pixar strongly believes that innovation does not happen on WhatsApp, Facebook or via email conversations.

SETTING THE SCENE

WHO typically is involved in teambuilding?

- Often teams are formed by management gathering some people together and then hoping that they somehow find a way to work together and create value for the company.
- In more hierarchical command and control organizations teams often rely on management and HR to support them with teambuilding.
- It is a cliché, but in Agile organizations every team member is responsible for team building.
- Teams that take ownership of their own development have a higher chance of becoming a high performing team.

YOU WILL LEARN:

> **Visual Collaboration Techniques**
Team way of dealing/working with preferences
Team personalities
Team feedback
Team development

WHEN and where does teambuilding occur?

- In many traditional organizations teambuilding is considered an annual event that often takes place outside of the office.
- Stereotyped old-fashioned teambuilding events involve a bowling alley and a steakhouse. In organizations that are built around high performing teams teambuilding is a recurring activity. For example in organizations where teams practice Agile Scrum a team retrospective is part of every sprint (2 weeks).
- These organizations often have created facilities and safe environments for teams to hold retrospectives and focus on team development.

WHAT happens when you are teambuilding?

During teambuilding activities or retrospectives teams try to do one or a combination of the following things to ultimately become high performing teams:

- Discover ways of dealing with preferences within teams.
- Get to know each other and understand personalities within teams.
- Share individual feedback on team performance.
- Sketch target conditions for the team and agree on ways to improve team performance.

CELEBRATING TEAM ACCOMPLISHMENT

VISUAL COLLABORATION TECHNIQUES

You have been part of multiple teams within your company. The performance of teams that you were part of varied significantly. You wonder why some teams were more productive than others. Also you wonder why everybody within those teams quickly seemed to have found a way to work together effectively. You are looking for good practices and initiatives that you could propose to your team members. The following visual thinking and collaboration techniques could enable you and your team to become high performing teams.

TEAM WAY OF DEALING/ WORKING WITH PREFERENCES

- The way that individuals work together in teams is not always aligned with what all individuals prefer. There is a quick and simple way to find out how individuals within your team would like to work together.
- Organize your team in a room and ask everybody to think for themselves: what makes us high; and what keeps us low?
- Visualize these preferences on a flip and start a team dialogue to see where you can change the way you work together.
- If you are worried that people will have difficulty expressing themselves you could structure the process by asking them which things they do or do not like on specific topics:
  A. The way the team plans and allocates work.
  B. The way the decisions are taken within the team.
  C. The way the team shares information.
  D. Etc.

TIP: Becoming a high performing team starts with recognizing that different things motivate different people.

TEAM PERSONALITIES

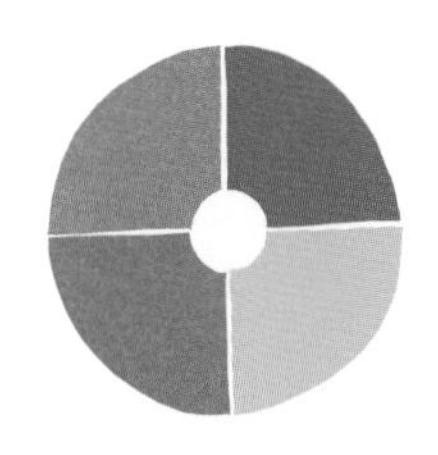

- There are many ways to identify different personalities within your team such as Big5, Myers-Briggs, and the Color Coding system.
- We have very good experiences with the DISC personality tests (based on William Marston and developed by Walter Clarke) and how teams can use them to understand their members and dynamics.
- The DISC test measures 4 quadrants of personality (Dominance, Influence, Steadiness and Conscientiousness) for each individual team member.
- By plotting the outcome of the test for each individual on a team charter you have a great overview of the diversity within your team. Based on the team charter you can start a dialogue on what is needed to become a high performing team.

TIP: For teams that are looking for a quick and less sophisticated assessment, taking an animal quiz can be useful and fun at the same time. Find out who is the lion, elephant, monkey or snake within the team.

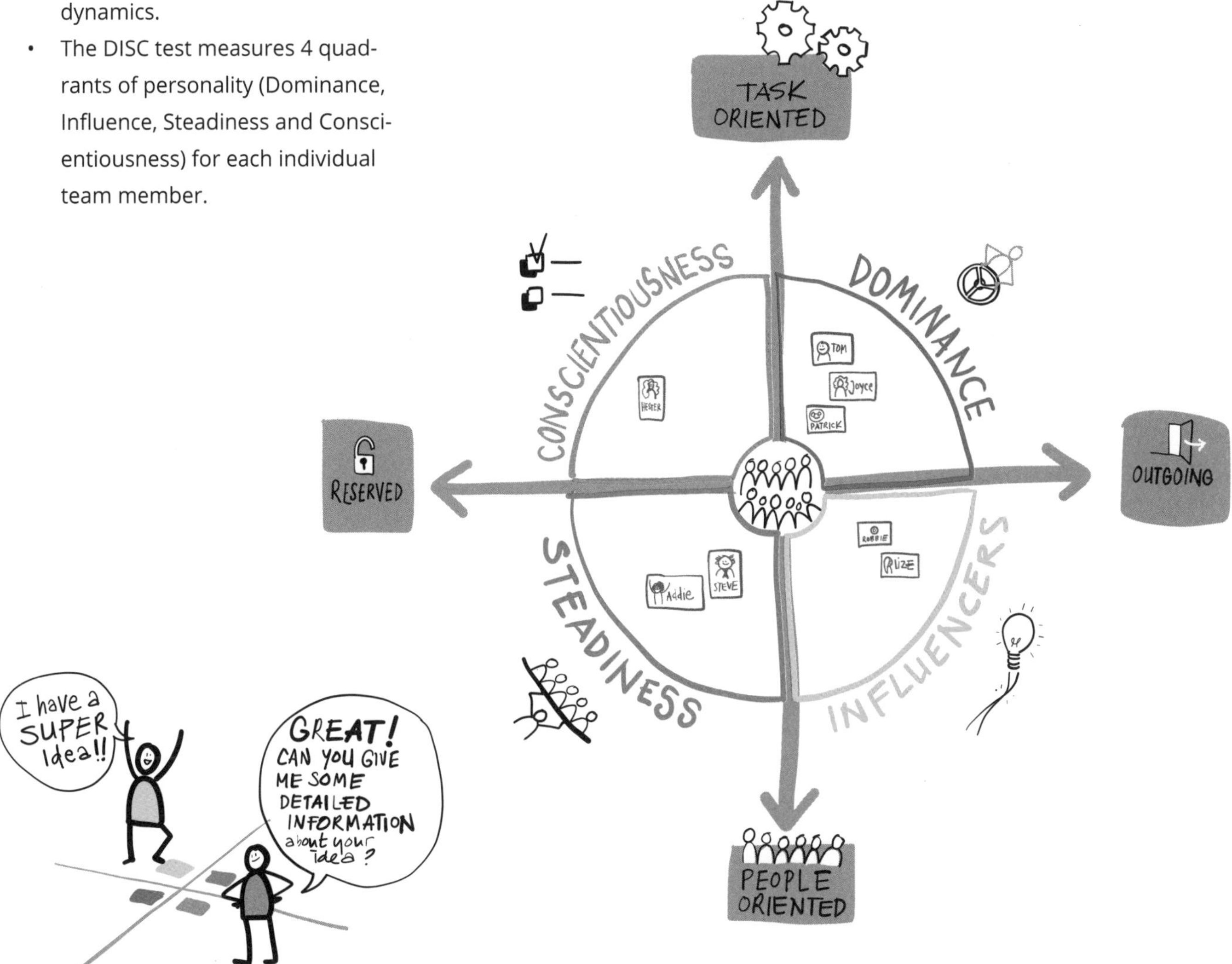

TEAM FEEDBACK

- Many books, articles and blogs have been written on why giving fast and frequent feedback is important for teams.
- We would like to suggest three simple and fun ways to share feedback within teams using visual thinking techniques:
  A. Ask everybody within your team which things they loved, appreciated or found frustrating during the past couple days or weeks. Let them capture on a flipchart what they believe the team should start, stop or keep doing.
  B. Check the team temperature by having everybody plot their avatar next to a thermometer on a flipchart. Individuals who are under pressure or too busy will be "hot" while individuals who are stuck or feel left out will be "cold".
  C. Play a card game, where each card has both a positive and negative statement on topics related to team performance, way of working, mindset and behavior. By holding up green, amber or red signs all team members indicate whether they sympathize more with the positive or negative statements.

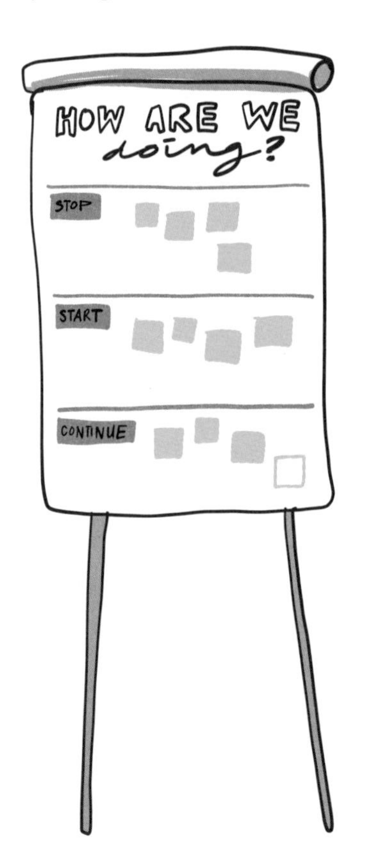

TEAM DEVELOPMENT

- For teams that are looking to take ownership and actively work on becoming high performing teams we would like to refer to the concept of "Improvement Themes" from Toyota Kata.
- Based on team feedback the team collectively decides upon an improvement theme.
- In four steps the team agrees on the first steps they will undertake to improve:
  A. Use sticky notes to come to a shared understanding of the current situation.
  B. Create a definition of awesome by asking the team how "the world" ideally would look.
  C. Describe the next target condition. This is the first realistic goal in the journey to becoming awesome.
  D. Identify the first possible steps you can take as a team to realize the target condition and decide upon frequency and follow-up discussions.

BENEFITS:

- Discover team member individual preferences.
- Get a better understanding of team dynamics.
- Share feedback faster and more frequently.
- Activate your team to become a high performing team.

THERE ARE NO SHORTCUTS
to becoming a
HIGH PERFORMING TEAM

SHUT UP AND DRAW

5. KEEP IT UP! ENDING IS BEGINNING

Congratulations! You've reached the end of this book, now it's up to you to start a new chapter of your own as you weave your new-found visual thinking and collaboration skills into the fabric of your daily work. It might initially feel a little strange when you start drawing at work, let alone sharing your visual notes with colleagues. But all great things grow from small beginnings. You have planted the seed of a new visual thinker. Now watch yourself grow as you practice and practice to hone your skills. You'll get quicker. You'll get better. You'll flip the visual switch in your brain. As you grow in confidence you can start sharing your visuals. Visual thinking will begin to come to you so naturally that you will have no trouble showing off your skills in real-time business settings. Your drawings will help you make more of an impression in meetings – this is visual impact at work! Members of your team will follow your lead and start picking up pens and pencils as they experience the power of visualizing ideas. In some companies we've worked with, people have formed visual thinking communities, working together to develop and embed this vital skill into their workflows. Once this ball is rolling, it takes on a momentum of its own. The expansion of visual thinking takes center stage. It can evolve fast; from visual collaboration within teams to teams that have the power to visually convince management and ultimately to teams that visually co-create new products with customers. We call this the visual journey, a path that empowers people and organizations to make maximum use of the creativity inherent in us all.

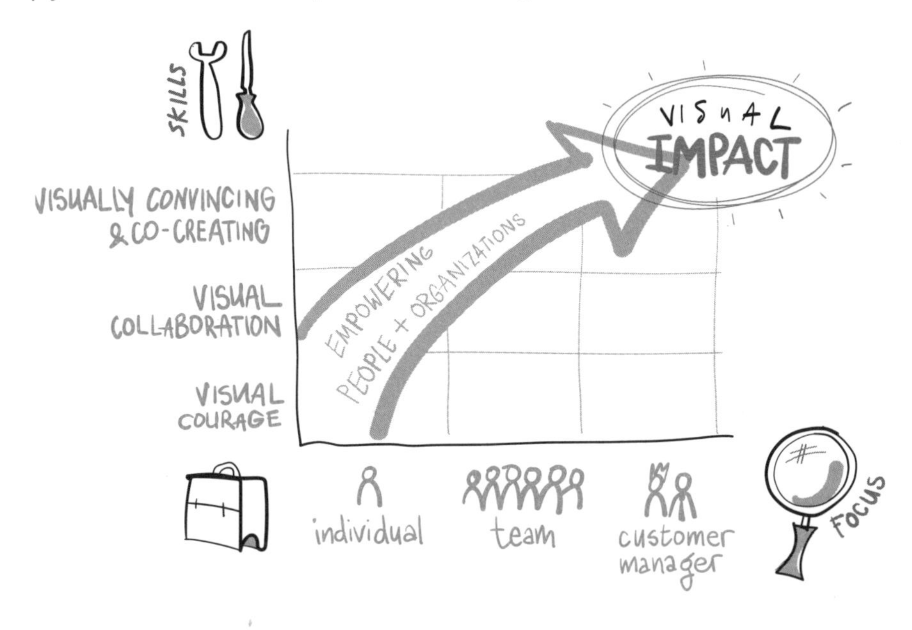

5.1 TIPS

The more you practice, the better you get. It's that simple. Your confidence will grow. You'll dare to draw for a wider audience. If you continue down this path, you'll end up making real visual impact.

Draw every day. Keep practicing! You can use your skills at home. Make an invitation, a birthday card, a to-do list.

Choose a color palette ahead of time. Make sure you have yellow (customer/purpose), gray and black. Other colors can come from the palette of your client or your own business.

Don't use too many colors. Your drawing will end up looking like a child's picture.

Buy a sketchbook and a beautiful case to hold your favorite pens and markers. Practice (did we mention practicing already?) Build up your own gallery of icons.

Share! Show each other icons and visual ideas in a business setting.

TIP: Don't set the bar too high. It doesn't have to be perfect. Imperfections stick in the memory and encourage people to cooperate on further developing an idea.

REMEMBER: it's all about communicating!

Make your (drawing) life easy. Get your flips ready before a meeting; draw a frame and a title banner.

After a meeting (in your own time, without other people around) make a sketch note or visual summary of the meeting. Send this to the participants by email or in a WhatsApp group.

Suddenly suffering from "sketcher's block" in a meeting? Talking and drawing at the same time is tough. Break out by asking a colleague: How would you draw this?

Invite colleagues to draw with you: Have them make their own drawings on sticky notes.

If you snap a photo with your phone, use a filter to make it pop! The iPhone Chrome filter is great.

Make your photos square. This makes them easier to use in a PowerPoint or email. Think Instagram!

TIP: Make photos that zoom in on details of your drawings on a flip chart or your sketchbook.

Follow people who inspire you on social media.

#GRAPHICRECORDING
#VISUALCOLLABORATION
#VISUALTHINKING
#SKETCHNOTES
#VISUALREPORTING
#HANDWRITING
#GRAPHICFACILITATION
#BUSINESSDRAWING
#VISUALSTORYTELLING

The Office Lens app is great for taking photos. The app turns pictures into pdf files, fits them into an A4 format and overexposes them a bit which looks great as the whites will be closer to real white.

Paper 53 is a great app for sketching and drawing. It lets you draw in layers so you can, for example, draw on a photograph with a white brush.

If you want to draw something but just don't know where to start, check out **www.thenounproject.com**

5.2 ABOUT THE AUTHOR

WILLEMIEN BRAND

Willemien Brand has turned her passion for drawing and design into her life's work. She graduated with distinction from the prestigious Design Academy Eindhoven and enjoyed an award-winning career as an industrial designer with ATAG before setting up the successful visual communication company Buro BRAND with its labels Studio BRAND, BRAND Academy and BRAND Business. The longer she worked in design, the clearer it became to Willemien that drawing and visual thinking are powerful tools that can break down complex problems, engage employees and build bridges between businesses and their customers. Now she shares this passion with companies throughout the world as one of the leading figures in the visual communication revolution.

5.3 WITH ESSENTIAL INPUT FROM

PIETER KOENE

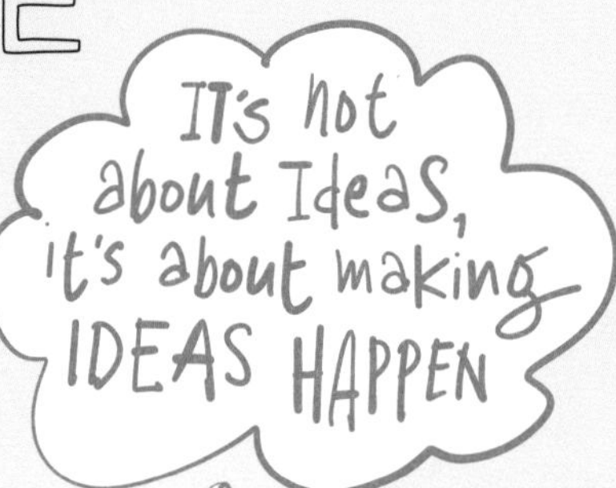

IT'S not
about Ideas,
it's about making
IDEAS HAPPEN

Pieter is an experienced business professional with 16 years consulting experience of which the last 13 years at PwC. As Consulting Lead Partner for one of PwC's key clients he has a proven track record of working with management teams on a broad range of strategic and operational questions. His main expertise is the design and realisation of value propositions and operating models. For Pieter, visual thinking is a vital tool for collecting data and stimulating cooperation focused on solving problems and identifying opportunities and innovative solutions. In New York he won a global Award of The Association of Management Consulting Firms for Excellence in Consulting.

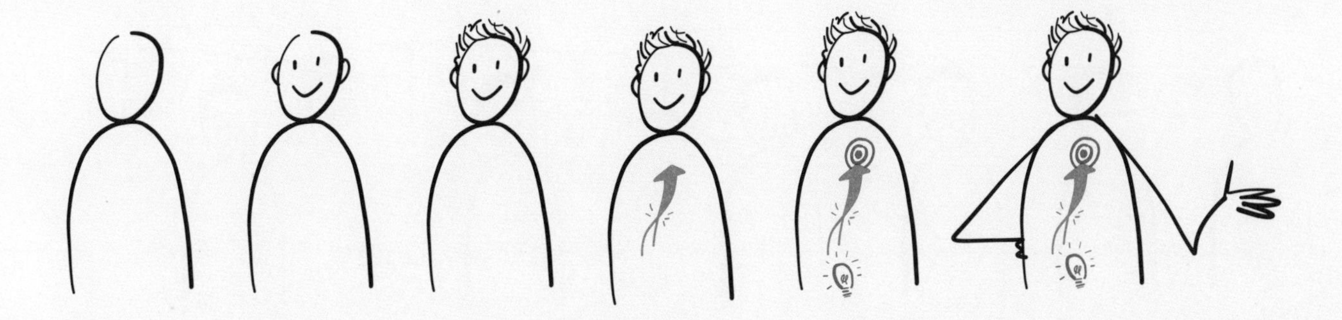

MARTIJN ARS

Martijn is a Senior Manager at PwC Consulting. He holds a MSc degree in Engineering and a postgraduate executive MSc in Finance. He is a certified Agile Scrum product owner and SAFe 4.0 practitioner. With his background in engineering he is programmed to design innovative solutions for complex problems and design thinking is hard-wired into his brain. In the past 10 years he applied these skills in various business settings as advisor in the banking industry. Together with his clients he has designed value propositions that better address customer needs and implemented operating models that execute core banking processes faster.

PIETER VERHEIJEN

CATCH THE NEXT WAVE BEFORE IT CATCHES YOU

Pieter is a Senior Manager at PwC with 10 years of consulting experience. His passion is helping clients to innovate their business models and stay relevant into the future. For him, visual thinking is the ideal way to collaborate effectively in teams and connect the dots to shape new solutions. Pieter is part of PwC's Future of Banking team and actively analyzes the latest trends in the market. He has a keen interest in the rise of FinTech companies and Pieter has a wealth of expertise in developing business models, partnerships and ecosystems.

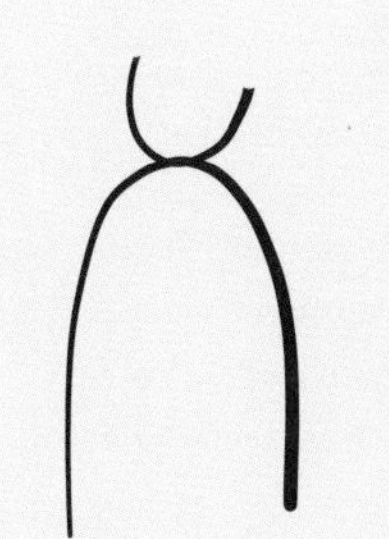

5.4 OUR FAVORITE BOOKLIST

Left to right, top to bottom: The Sketchnote Handbook by Mike Rohde, Game Storming by Dave Gray, Sunni Brown and James Macanufo, Bikablo 1 from Neuland, Event Design handbook by Roel Frissen, Ruud Janssen and Dennis Luijer, The Back of the Napkin by Dan Roam, Visual Metaphors Inspirational Workbook by Dario Paniagua, Man meets Woman by Yang Liu, The Doodle Revolution by Sunni Brown, Hand-Lettering for Everyone by Cristina Vanko, Creative Confidence by Tom & David Kelley, Draw Your Own Alphabets by Tony Seddon, Business Model Generation by Alex Osterwalder and Yves Pigneur, Visual Meetings by David Sibbet, Drawing Book: Make a World by Ed Emberley.

5.5 HOW THIS BOOK WAS DONE

We owe a huge thank you to Bionda from BIS Publishers for encouraging us to write this book. Thanks also to our interns Jessica van der Ende, Isabelle van Eijsden and Sophie de Ruiter. Thank you Hugo Seriese and Inge de Fluiter for your valuable brainstorming and reviewing.
And a special thanks to the people below, who helped in countless ways. We are eternally grateful for having such a great team supporting us.

All illustrations in this book were done on a 12,9-inch iPad Pro with an Apple Pencil.

We used the Adobe Illustrator Draw app, in this way the sketch appeared immediately after uploading on the Imac desktop Adobe Illustrator CC application.

Portraits we made in the Adobe Photoshop Sketch app.

We used the following fonts:
Montserrat
Helveticamazing
Open Sans
American typewriter

FROM THE SAME AUTHOR

VISUAL DOING

Visual Doing will improve your visual craftsmanship and broaden your skillset. It's a practical and accessible handbook for incorporating visual thinking into your daily business and communication.

The author leads you through a new range of exercises, techniques and subjects which will help you to tell your own visual story. It takes a look at these subjects from different perspectives: 'me as an individual', 'we as a team' and 'us as a company.' It helps you to clarify complex information, pitch innovative strategies and foster a visual culture within your organization.

VISUAL THINKING & DOING WORKBOOKS

The Visual Thinking and Visual Doing workbooks are great tools to help you kick-start your visual journey and gain confidence to produce amazing compelling drawings.

Crammed with tons of visual exercises, ranging from tracing illustrations to drawing hacks. These workbooks will inspire you to design and share your own icons! (really it will!)